To Beloved Bea,
Forever,
Zoe

M000096592

# LOVE SONGS

for

# SKY CHILDREN

A COLLECTION OF POETRY AND FREE VERSE

by

# WESLEY BUNIGER

ENDEAVOR ACADEMY
*Certum Est Quia Impossibile Est*

*Time is*
*Too slow*
*For those*
*Who wait*

*Too long*
*For those*
*Who grieve*

*Too short*
*For those*
*Who laugh*

*But for those*
*Who truly love*
*Time*
*Does not exist*

- David and Linda La Flamme

This collection is dedicated to Manasa Ocelia
Because she loves me,
And to all who are Endeavor Academy.

My eternal gratitude
To everyone, including
Dear One, Charlotte, Miriam and
Jubi; Stryder and Pearl Buniger

Love Songs for Sky Children
*A Collection of Poetry and Free Verse by Wesley Buniger*

International Standard Book Number (ISBN-10): 1-890648-90-6

(ISBN-13): 978-1-890648-90-9

Library of Congress Control Number: 2010935461

Published By:
Endeavor Academy
501 East Adams Street, Wisconsin Dells, WI 53965, USA
Phone: +1 608-253-1447
www.endeavoracademy.com
Email: publishing@endeavoracademy.com

COVER PAINTING: *Friday 13th  Speed Limit Six Minutes* BY WESLEY BUNIGER

# Contents

# Little Bird In My Heart

et's go into the wilderness
Where I freely blend in.
The hurry of this busy street
Is no place for you.
The madness of city life
Tangles your pretty hair
And tries unsuccessfully
To dull your sense of wonder.
I want to show you how to find comfort
In a cozy hollow
Or upon a grassy hill.
Let us sleep together
Where the deer bed down
And in the morning
Swim under a waterfall
With the fishes. *in the trees*
(6) I became a tree ~~once~~. *or the trees*
It lasted but a short while.
The experience had to do with
My need of salvation.
From loneliness and confusion
(1) I reached out and blessed
(2) Each tree in ~~that part of~~ the great forest.
Also the ground and patches of blue sky overhead.
(3) I ~~felt~~ *felt* the trees respond warmly.
I sat down upon a small boulder
Next to a strong young tree
Growing out of a pile of rock.
A small spring emerged
Between its roots.

*(5) My skin turned to bark*
*small branches grew*
*from my sides*
*transformation nearing*
*complete*
*myself omersed*
*in the being of a*
*strong young tree*

The trickling voice sang small yet clear.
There I was with my face in my hands
Feeling sad and unfinished.
I closed my eyes.
④There was no breeze, yet a branch
Reached gently around my shoulder
And caressed my cheek with its needles.
I opened my eyes.
And there was my body sitting still.
My skin was turning into bark
And small branches were growing out of my sides.
The transformation was becoming complete
And it scared me.
I was looking at myself from the being
Of that strong young tree.
Quickly I moved back into my body.
The tree didn't want me to go
And I felt its heart break as I left.
With the spell broken in my mind
I realized the other trees had been singing.
They fell silent as my awareness faltered.
A small bird flew up and landed
Just across from me.
He proceeded to scold me for being afraid
And told me of time running out
For man.
My understanding crashed
And I could no longer comprehend
What the little bird was saying
As he hopped from branch to branch.
I felt ashamed and more
Frightened than ever
As the thoughts of the trees became
Wind in their leaves.
I said I was sorry and would try harder.
They forgave me.

I touched the strong young tree
On the branch realizing too late its spirit
Was pure
And begged forgiveness for my intrusion.
Small drops of sap appeared,
It cried for me.
Still, very frightened I sat on the rock.
The people I was with
Returned down the trail talking.
Even though I was in plain sight
They did not see me
Until they were right beside the boulder.
Stopping, they turned in surprise
Saying I was lost to them and they worried.
They were not people of the forest
And were not aware of the little bird.
He fell silent, waited nervously
A few moments
Then flew off disgusted at being ignored.
The afternoon had wore on
And the light in the sky
Began changing into evening gloam.
The others looking about askance
Wanted to hurry back to camp
And the glow of a warm fire.
They were quickly annoyed
At my lack of fear of the coming dark.
They didn't know I was safe
Among new friends.
Somehow, I found my legs
And moved off the boulder
To the waiting path
And followed them slowly
Back to the road.
I looked back at the strong young tree
Saying someday I would return.

Stumbling on the uneven surface
I moved around the bend losing sight
Of the place where the trees had found me.
Still dazed I realized something special
Had happened and vowed to grow
And be worthy of that working vision.

# Family Of All

The shining leaves in the summer trees
All dance with the sun, the summer leaves.
It reminds me so of His love for us all
I gather the words, a song for the fall.
Every small child has love in its heart
As each falling leaf, knows when to depart.
And even though snow falls down on below
It can't cover love there, that which I know.
Gifted with song I fly through the sky
To gladden the hearts, of all that pass by.
It matters not which song I may sing
With love in my heart,
It's the coming of spring.
And with the summer's return to valley and hill
The heartbeat of love continues on still.

CHORUS

Give us to love
Give us to life
Give us to man
Give us to wife
Bless us this day
The glory we know
Show us the way
We want to grow.

Thank you for grace
Thanks for your hand
Thank you for love
And for the land.

We give to you
Our will in return
Love is to share
As we all learn.

Now in the glow of our summer's delight
We dance with our moon, the way is in sight.
Mother Earth turns around with fall on her brow
Everyone sees, what love can do now.
With winter's snow filling the skies
Ice dancers glow, filling our eyes.
The Creator creates in our dream from above
A bounty of stars, and space for all love.
Spring blossoms bursting with color gone wild
I'm glad to step forward, as nature's new child.

CHORUS

Give us to rebirth
Keep us for good
Show us the way
To right livelihood.
Keep us all straight
Stand tall in the sun
Blend us together
Make us all one.

Send out the word
Universe far and near
Tell all we have joined
For now we are clear.
Touching You now
We learn of each other
It's joyful to say
Both sister and brother.

ALL CHANT

With all of the wings that fly in the sky
With all of the fins that swim in the sea
With all of the feet that walk in the way
With all of the roots that grow in the earth
With all of the love that fills up each heart
With all of the thought that spills from our eyes
With all of our being we cover the earth
With all of our strength we heal the hurt
And with all our songs we fill all of our souls,
So you, our Creator see below and above
A gladness that quickens
The wave of your love.

# Universe Jar

 love to listen to others sing
Their songs of love, joy does bring.
Not jealous I but glad to see
Another's way of growing free.
Each, they are unique their way
Join I them in weave today.

II
Let our hearts sing in loving song
Let our words kiss all life long.
Let our thoughts become as one
Let our deeds outshine the sun.

III
The moon glows down all around
Lightning strikes from cloud to ground.
I learn yet again to step in flow
Like waterfall, to pool below.
With all there is to see and do
Can't feel anything without You.

IV
Let's be together evermore
Let us sail love's ship to shore.
Let us always in love be
Let us nest our young to lea.

V

Continue to grow in love's glowing light
Nurture the young and old alike.
Make our way slow, slow back home
Skim fleecy cloud and scudding foam.
Rise after resting yet once more
Gain threshold of perfection's airtight door.
Our charge is to become that which we are
Not even confined to universe jar.

# This My World

ong bill quick wing
Dance before my eyes
Regal plumage glistens
Sun in summer skies

She whom I search for
Draws closer to my heart
Long bill carry dream to her
A smile for a start

He say I good for her
She is good for me
Love grows flower like
Sapling into tree

Forest life crowds around
Here to wish us well
Animals all know so much
Ancient story do they tell

Song of sunny deeds
Like thunders roar at night
GOD'S face in clouds abound
Rains fall to my delight

Moon wax large to full
Eyes watch cat below
I spy her on rolling hill
Honey loves to flow

Make I ready here
Strong yet humble nest
Glad tidings to prepare
For I am truly blessed

Good come to me easily
Though the wait often long
Now have I ideal life
Love's a heartfelt song

Singing shatter sadness
Who is quick to go away
Negatore shadow shrink
Love is here to stay

Brave eye open gaze about
Fragrance fill the air
Pardon me my stupid look
I cannot help but stare

It's you see I at last
Heart go wild in me
You feel so good to know
Love I your company.

Now is time to say
To you I pledge my life
This my world
Please come inside
And be my loving wife

# Foot In The Door

any years
A gleaming flashlight
Laying on the floor
Pointing nowhere
In particular.
Slowly learn to see
While Truth permeates
Moving to realize
As snow melts
All around
Foot in the door.

II
Floating now
Above the ground
With nowhere to go,
Except inside.
Time soon to heal others,
Blend the wounds of sorrow
With serenity's peace
Sing our song completely
With foot further in the door.

III
Quietly in summer
A spring
Trickles over stones
Beneath my roots.
The earth is moist
Moss is soft, cool

---

To touch
The boulder we lean on
Leans on us.
Singing bird hears
Our attention.
Others interrupt
Panic unknown.
Foot in door fading.


IV
Wander lost
Across empty landscape
Among bones of denial
Accepting even failure
As a lesson.
Shadows of insecurity
Ply their trade
With wispy blindfolds
Tripping up thoughts
As they try to leave
Long twisted tunnel.
To no avail
The waves of inertia ebb
At what is left of our being.
Lifting our hearts
With snail like movements
The light of memory
Shines on our soul.
With grace,
Foot still in door.


V
Ever grateful we take
Time out from youth
As others fill
Those spaces with exuberance.

The leaves of our lives
Swirl about our feet
On the afternoon trail.
Knee above foot in the door.

## VI

Long is the journey
Many are the lifetimes needed.
Learn how to drown
In all there is
To drink from.
Patiently, still
Unable to heal others
Can't see end of the line...
Anxiously skirting anxiety...
Remember your center
You are doing just fine.
Losing more stones
That you carry
Lets shoulder above knee
With foot in the door.

## VII

Just a gentle move
Now
And the rest glides through.
To help the others of me,
We leave
A foot in the door.

# Show The Way

I wakened early
Before first light
My dreams give way
To heart's delight.
Seeing you
Sound asleep
Gives one moment
Beyond all keep.
Your shining beauty
And soulful eyes
Clear all clouds
From tall blue skies.
Winter arrives
On heels of fall
I snuggle close
Your beck'n call.
Safe in your heart
Feel the beat
My animal wild
Kiss your feet.
With the birds
Sing you song,
I am amazed,
All day long.
All your love
You gladly give
Infinite storehouse
Is your sieve.

Throughout the day
My mind on you
I walk the path
Straight and true.
Work the wood
Be the grain
Love the life
Unknot the pain.
As evening strolls
From around the hill
My shadow stalks
Your door and sill.
Both warmth
And song
Crackling fire
Welcome kiss
Your heart's desire.
Hold you long
Drink you deep
Love for you
Cannot sleep.
Your silken arms
Around my neck
And waist
From truth and light
All fears are chased.
Grow I, in your love
Each  passing day,
Your graceful
Strengths
Show the way.

# HerSelf Love I

he is all
And then some.
The curve of
Her flowing line
Matches easily
Even the greatest tide.
Each eve the
Faded glow
Calls me to her.
Lay I down
The labor done.
Glad, my feet
Find the way
To our door;
And with a gentle kiss
Upon her brow
I'm given away
To peace.
With sparkling eyes
And arm around my side
She holds me close
In her heart's
Open glow.
No fire
Can match her light
No word
Can justice do.

She, has prepared
A meal
Of simple call,
Filled with love's
Patient caress.
Dine I kingly
With my beloved
While warmth of hearth
Does burnish
Knees and toes,
Face and shin.
We sing our songs
Amid bursts of laughter
Music made fine
By her golden soul.
On into the night with
Kitten curled in her lap
We gaze into each other's eyes
Touch hearts
While holding hands.
With compassion's power
To transform
We are set free,
As cock's crow finds her
Asleep in my arms
Before the embers.

# Dragon's Walk

ight wind
Blowing
Fresh
Blue sky
Spring day
Around
To my door
As cotton ball
Clouds
Ease over
The southern
Hills
And skirt
The valley
Below.
My life
Is as always
Each day
A view
Of the moment
Now learned
To be aware
In the present
Only
Now I know
It too.
The trees
Outside
My window
Bend in the

Breeze
But I see
They are
Really
Waving to me
Saying
Glad to see
You made it
Welcome
Here into
Our hearts
Welcome
Home.
We love you
For taking
Care of us
Each twig
And leaf
Is yours
To keep
As we share
The cycles
Of this now.
Sunlight
Dances in
Our branches
Just for you
Beloved child
Full of grace
We watched you
Understand
Your self
Felt love open
Up your heart
And calm the
Hot flame

Of confusion.
The words
Of another's
Teaching
Put it all
Together
As you
Heard the
Truth
And saw
Yourself
Watching you
Through your
Own eyes.
It was
Your inner
Being behind
Your brow
And all
Your years
Felt good
As memory
Came back
Into your
Heart,
We watched
You
Check in
With your
Inner Self
Again
Like old
Friends
Meeting
At a rural
Cross road

The wise
Inner Being
Smiled
At your
Touch of
Comprehension
And you
Knew again
He had
Been there
All along.
The echoes
Of the words
Are faded now
But you are
Strong
At last
For they
Touched
That place
Inside
You call
Home
You felt
The surge
Of all
Knowing
At last
It spread
Throughout
Your body
This tiny
Quiet ripple
That washed
Up on the
Shores of

All your
Questions
And washed
Away
The tears
Of all your
Fear
And all the
Other
Loving's touch
That had
Been left
Out.
Dragged
Kicking
And screaming
Into
Your birth
This life
You now
Understand
And
Remember
Why it is
You came back
Again,
You are
One of
The swans
Who fly
Free.
Love
Is your
Destination
Only
Now you

Never
Have
To leave
Home
In your
Beloved
Wilderness
Where
Loneliness
Is never
Alone.


<u>II</u>
The long
Flowing
Beautiful hair
Of joy
Withstands
Time's test
Of brush
And comb.
We all
Come here
To nest
Eventually
For there
Is no other
Like it
No peaceful
Coexistence
Within
Or without.
All your
Children
Know this
Before they

Too
Are covered
Up by
The hurry
Of illusion
Like us
Let the
Instinct to
Kill your
Television
Prevail
Tune in
Instead
To the music
Of your soul
And be aware
Of just who
Put it there
With you.
You
And your
Wilderness
Are one
And the same.

## III

Feeling
The joy
Return
To my heart
I step into
Life's dance
And take
Up song
Lending my
Inner strength

To the
Procession
Of stars
All the
While
Observing
What grace
Does for
Timing;
For it is
So easy
To miss
This great
Ride.
I must
Tell the
Others
Yet in
The dark–
Better yet
Show them
By being
Happy
In the moment.
Let them observe
Me seeing
Myself
Watching
All that
I am
And loving
Every
Minute
Of it.
Magicians
Are they

Who can
Transform
Limitation
Into endless
Creation;
What fun
Getting
Caught
Pulling
It off.

IV
A puppy's
Smile
Though
Silent
And close
To the floor
Still fills
The room
With light.
My fingers
Nibbled
And cheek
Licked
For salt
Of tears
Now gone
Assures me
That I am
This present
Awareness
Proven
Without
Demonstration;
Just a

Warm hearted
Knowing
Inside
That connects
Me with
My own
Personal
Inner strength
Which
Surfaces a
New
Self confident
Smile.

V
Light
Reflected
In the night
Sky
From the
Sparkling horde
Takes on
A whole
New
Intensity
For now
I see each
Bright point
As its own
Master of compassion
Complete
Within
The realm
Of my
Knowing
It is this

That makes
The whole
More than
The sum
Of its parts.
Awareness
In the
Present
Observed
With the
Inner being
Is the breath
Of the stone
That before
Appeared
To just
Lay there
In the mud.

<u>VI</u>
The soul of
This
Mother Earth
Breathes
With myriad
Activity
Accompanied
By her
Countless
Children,
Who each
Dances to
Rhythms
Peculiar
Only to
Those who

Are yet to touch
The inside
Of themselves.

## VII
Slowly with care
Do I take up
The herald
Unfamiliar
With the
Élan of
Experience
Yet wonder
Struck
The flagstaff
In my hands
Feels familiar
As all of me
Knows
It belongs there.

## VIII
Marching along
With endless
Others
I drift off
To sleep
Among
The dreams
Waiting
To be made
Manifest
Their
Unformed
Coachwork
Dazzling

The eye
Of a giddy
Heart
As the
Resplendent
Teams are
Fleshed out
And harnessed
To the traces.
The music
Yet to be invented
Courses
Through the veins
Of our great
Composer
Blasting
The patina
Of conventional
Wisdom
As even
Grim Reaper
Takes a back seat,
Content
To be a spectator
For a change.
In the
Early morning
Hours
All is finally
Made ready.
Parade Master
Gives the
Signal
And overalled
Helper
Pulls the

Chock
Holding back
The lead
Wheel.

IX
At first
Only a faint
Patter
With tentative
Chorus
Preambles
The main
Course
As billions
Of brothers
And sisters
All chime in.
Every available
Cloud
Is pressed
Into service.
Overcrowded
And rubbing
Shoulders
Their laughter
Booms across
The valley
As lightening
Signals
Drought
At an end.

X
Wind is
Back sharp,

Prying fingers
To the calm.
Stepped
Lightening
Reveals
The rattled
Dust
As it rises up
Only to be
Crushed
By the
Watery
Onslaught
Much the same
As myself
Falling back
Into old
Patterns of
Forgetfulness.
The stinging wet
Shock
Rekindles
Memory
Of a greater
Knowing
As body
Saunters
Under roof
Already soaked
With freezing
Shame.
Saddened
Heart
Still broken
By life's
Latest

Escapade
Wondering
If change
Of plot
Will ever
Come in
To rescue
The hero
Who wasn't
So strong
After all.
All there is
On any
Horizon
Is asking
For light
From the
Source
Inside
Learning
You can't find
Any of Your
Own
Out there.
Slowly
Again
One more
Time
I start over
Intending
To bring
Errant child
Back home
To now's
Understanding.
The Inner

Being
Is there
Waiting with
A heartfelt
Smile
To heal
The fingers
And toes
And every
Other part
Of the
Fallen
Weeping child.

## XI
The vision said
The last of the
Journey
Was only a
Little way
More
Yet the
Impossible
Would be
Possible to
Accomplish.

## XII
The terror
And withering
Fear of
Being left
Behind
Was speared
By
Determination

To succeed
Somehow.
Remembered now,
This was the
First lesson
Of inner
Strength
Heartsick
At having
Been so stupid
As to forget
The Creator
In the
First place.
With continued
Careful study
And incessant
Restart at true
Self forgiveness
Refinding my
Inner Being
Who is my
Only connection
Home
I begin again
With silence
This joyful journey
Known as
Dragon's Walk.

# Moonglow For R.D.

iesta
Voices
Rhythm
Hands,
Tapping
Toes and
Smiling
Fans,
With touching
Hearts
All know
The steps
This
Lifeful
Dance,
This
Dance
Of life.
Your
Plumage
Bright
With bells
A ring
Breath
Of life
On pipes
All sing;
My true
One
Hears

Your love
Feels
The love
You bring.
Big, round,
Yellow moon,
Shines
Upon your
Midnight
song.
Her glow
Fills
The space
Between,
The thoughts
Where
We belong;
That restful
Place,
Where
Peace,
Is found
And hurry,
Sloughs
Along.
I am the
Little one
Inside
A great
Big hollow
Body,
Bouncing
Off the walls
Upside
Down and
Turning

All around,
Smile
So dreamtime
Slowly.
Feasting
Banquets
Fit for Kings
Piles of
Golden
Emerald
Rings;
Endless
Journeys
To and fro,
To this
I say
So what...
Stay home
With
Universe
Inside
And let
The
Sidetrips
Go.
For I am
Already
The glitter
The mud
The song
The life;
The hurry,
Going slow.
When I'm
The wind
I see

Your thoughts
Your secrets
Don't you
Know;
I carry
Your words
From
Ear to ear
Though
You whisper
Soft and low.
The mighty
Torrent
May drown
Your voice
And hide
Your eyes
Away
So I just
Slide
Around
Your
Lovely waist
And hear
Your body
Say;
Come here
Go away
Do this
Do that
Please
Love me
Right away
You wish
You could
But hold me

Close
While
Lonely
Slips away.
So
Here I am
Your own
True love,
Your
messenger
In the night.
No more
You roam
Alone
For our
Love
Does make
It right.
Please
Kiss me
Now
And hold
Me close
Our love
Not fade
Away.
Once
Empty arms
Now
Full of you
Sing
Warm hearts
Here
To stay.
Your life
Do I share;

This night –
Our song –
The moon
So bright –
This moment
Without
Care.
Let us
Drown
Ourselves
In love
Of life
And live
Eternal
Afterglow;
Our crashing
Tides
Do ebb
And flow
Our currents
Fathoms make,
And others
Share
The light
And joy
Trailing
In our wake.
We'll
Cast our net
And catch
The stars
Then gently
Let them go.
The comets
Too
I'll chase

For you;
Just to see
Where they
Do go.
With
Hearts
Content
We'll let
Our minds
Run free,
To pay
Attention
To all
The little
Things
Floating
In the
Sea.
No heavy
Cargo
Of past
Forlorn
Shall
We carry
In our
Hold,
Nor icy
Anchor
Of fear
Concealed
To keep
Us in
The cold.
Our truth
Our love
Our being

Close
Is that
Which
Prevails,
And
Forever more
The breath
Of life
Will billow
In our sails.
And when
Our
Spacefaring
Days
Be done
With a
Final island
At our
Bow,
You'll find me
Along side
Your gilded
Hull
All randy
With you
Still.

# Journey's Brocade

low gypsy
At home
Among
Wandering leaves
Your beautiful
Mother divine
No longer
Grieves.
Stone mountain
Resolve
She grows
Toward
Her next rung
Evolutions call
Ever so strong
Answering souls
Ever so young


II
This valley's
Trees
Bend in the
Rain
Though wind
Can be cruel
They never
Complain.
All lift up
Their hearts
In storm tossed

Refrain
Branches swinging
To tempos
None can explain.

## III
Fresh
Dragonfly's wings
Unfolded to dry
Moonlight
Sparkles on water
He's ready,
Goodbye.

## IV
Make
This moment
Your own
Discover
Your song
Pour your
Heart into
Where you
Belong.
Go ahead,
Blaze a
Non linear
Trail;
Always, pioneers
Never can win
If they don't
Fail.

<u>V</u>
It's very
Interesting
This time
Around
The battle's
For Self
Not for
The ground.
Or, is the
Self
Foundation
Finally found?
Ultimate linkup
To family crowned.

<u>VI</u>
Of all the
Dimensions
I like
Zero
The best,
It's the
Beginning
Of all
And last
Of the rest.
Remember
The magic
To you befall
Especially now
When three
Turns to
Four.

VII
Surrender
Your kindness,
To all
You receive
Render your
Humble,
In Spirit
Believe.

VIII
With precious
Manasa
Blend
Celebration
With harmony,
Our jubilant
Silence
Ripples the sea.

IX
Dreaming
Easy
In a restful
Mode
Irredess
Dragonfly
Clasps
My earlobe.
Hanging there,
Unafraid,
She whispers
Into my
Ear.
Thank you
For saving

My loved ones
Trapped
Behind glass,
Thank you
For helping
Snail, at
Hot road
Get passed.
Thank you
For your hand
At fallen
Nest;
I'm sent here
To thank you
From all
The rest.
It is you,
How did
I know?
The trees
Point you out
Wherever
You go.
You take
Their seeds
Newly fallen
To brown,
Plant each
One carefully
In God's
Hallowed
Ground.
Often,
You are
Just a dot
On far

Rolling plain
There
Where we
Grow
And help
To bring
Rain.
We all
Go together
Evolve
Unto God,
If you
Could see
We look
Like a flood.
An unending
Torrent of bliss
In our blood
Given to choose
Given a could.
The Unlimited
Entity
Of supreme
Intelligence
Lovingly
Waits
For us all;
Now listen
Closely,
Can you
Hear the call?
Our path
Is wide
So wide
There's
No place

To hide.
We lose
Our way
When
We fail,
To recognize
The Creator
In our
Own jail.
Forgive
Yourself
Let judgement
Fall in the sea
Bliss awaits
Those
Who allow
Freedom
To be.
Empty, Hollow of
Self important
Identification,
In quiet
Acceptance
Am I filled
With our
Master,
And all of
Creation.
All of creation
Fits inside
Of my being
That this
Is so
Is just
What I'm seeing.
I am it.
It is I.

X

All this I'm told
By friend
Dragonfly,
Today
Have I
Learned
There's no
Such thing,
As goodby;
Today
Have I
Learned
Both below
And above,
There is
No end to
Unconditional
Love.
By this
Understand,
Dreaming tonight
Of the beach
In a far away
Land,
I'll waken
Tomorrow
All covered
With sand.
When my own
Spiritual progress
Seems slow
Look inside
Just to see,
I'm but a flash
Next to one
Complete turn
Of our own
Galaxy.

# Mother River

tanding still
On top of
Blue ridge
Mother River
Below
Flowing under
Old bridge.

She curls along
In no particular
Hurry
Like water
Is a wont,
Without worry.

Run down
The hill
To be
At her side
Gaze
Bank to bank
Her womanly
Tide.

Standing naked
Before her
Moon isn't
Full yet
She mingles
My toes

Invites
To her wet.

Stepping in
To my knees
Night bird
Calls out
My name,
Song and
A breeze
Both are
The same.

Up to my waist
Water is chill
Small waves
Lap on the beach
Old man Willow
Is thrilled.
River Mother
She beckons
To follow
Her down,
At ease now
Remember
To breathe;
So I won't drown.

Laughing
Together
I blend at
Her touch
With cosmos
Divine
My home
Loved
So much.

Moonlight
Through
Branches
Overhanging
The stream,
Filters
A glow
To our
Depths
Like a
Dream.

Floating
At buoyant
Neutral
Depth,
Become
The waters
That flow
Through
Poor fisherman's
Net.

Rolling and
Turning
Cartwheels
Like seals
Is just how
Wonderful
Looking
It feels.

Up on the
Surface
Forked
Log

Casts a
Shadow
On sight,
Small
Turtle family
Is holding
On tight.

Reach for
The moon
Gasping
For air
Tickle their
Tummies
With
Watery flair.

Old papa T
Goes back
To sleep,
He knows
It's just me
Plumbing
The deep.

'Rascally clown'
Mother T
Is upset,
I've wakened
The kids
From sleep
They could
Get.

Now Mother T,
I'll tell
A story

To put them
Back down,
If you'll
Promise
To bury
That storm laden
Frown.

The young ones
All boisterous
Grab on
To my hair,
As I rock back
In a watery
Chair.

At first
We all listen
To night's
Country din
As I find
Front of a story,
Somewhere
To begin.

This tale
Is about
Turtles
And fishes
You see,
And all about
Their adventures
Upriver,
Far from
The sea.

There once was
And forever
Will be
A need for
Turtles
And fishes
Fresh born,
Caused by
The breath
That blows
The great
Horn.

Each of us
Births here
A lesson
To learn
An ongoing
Saga
We each
Take our
Turn.

With each
Success
Large and small
We polish
Ourselves
And answer
The call.

We all
Have a choice
To make
At each
Turn
Like learning

To flow;
In resistance
We burn.

Our goals
And desires
Intentions
Complete,
Outcome Control
We learn
To delete.

Between
Thoughts
Of the mind
We plant
Our best
Seed
Then await
The results
In timing
Take heed.

Each of us
Grows
By leaps
And then
Bounds
Hearing
And singing
Beautiful
Sounds.

With help
From our
Self
We learn

How to serve
With that which
We are,
And double
Our joy
More than
By far.

Setting
Up house
In the unknown,
Certainty
Reigns
With possibilities
Shown.

This unlimited
Creation
Allows us
Be free
Access all
That there is
In Loves
Maternity.

With effort
And struggle
We learn to allow
Ourselves all,
And at the end
Of our road
We Kingdom
Recall.

Know that
Love is
The engine
The most

Powerful energy
There is,
With no
Whys, buts
Or how to's;
IS, just
IS.

With space-time
Relative –
Thought
Is the swift,
Our minds
Are so
Powerful
Moments choice
Is a gift.

Ask in
Your heart
If a decision
Is good
For us all,
A feeling
Wellbeing
Is the
Right call.

On and on
Into the night
I regaled the True,
Until all
Eyes were closed
Except for
My two.
Gently,
I placed
Each Youngster

Back on the log
Kissed Mrs. T
And pushed off
In the fog.

I could hear
Wharf rats
Talking
As they chewed
On ropes
Wood and stays,
Attached to
Old boats
Tied up
In the Quays.

Their jargon
Was that
Of a rough
Rowdy lot
But I enjoyed
Their particular
Truth
Take it or not.

Mother River
Carried me
Along
In temperate
Ease
When off
In the
Distance
I heard
A small
Sneeze.

Then there
Was crying
And choking
Sounds,
Swimming up fast
A body
I found.

Lifting
Her head
Mired in
Wet hair
Moonlight
Revealed
A vacant
Cold stare.

Stroking
For shore
The beach
Did we make
I breathed
Into her mouth
But no breath
Would she take.

Feeling a pulse
I pushed under
Ribcage
Mother river
Spurt out
Of her mouth
In a terrible
Rage.

Turned
On her side
So she won't
Choke
Deaths grip

On this one
Was finally
Broke.
Sitting
Up slowly
I cradled
Under my arm
What I saw
To be lovely,
Undeserving
Of harm.

Crying real tears
She said
Her life
Was a mess,
She'd been
Through hell
And torn
Her new dress.

Between sobs
Saying her
World
Was so cruel,
Rough men
Wanted only
Her body
And she'd
Flunked
Out of
School.

So I decided
Right then
To tell her

The truth
She looked
In my eyes
And said
Her name's
Ruth.

I told her
About how
We put
Ourselves
Through,
All kinds
Of hoops
To see
What we do.

As soon as
We learn
Real Love of Self
Life will improve,
And self respect
Follows us
Into the
Groove.

I told her
About my life
How I turned
Black
Into blue,
Eventually
Fumbled
Into the Light,
Discovered
The Truth.

It wasn't
Easy
Sometimes
I regret,
But that
Is all
Passed now
The moment
Is set.

I improve
The future
By nurture
Me now
I live
The unknown
It's exciting
And how.

I told her
My job
Is to serve
And befriend,
That I could
Help,
Yes,
To that end.

She took
Me up
On my offer
No strings,
Already her
Strength
Bloomed
Her heart
It took wing.

I continued
To counsel
Truth's easy Path
Easy because
There's no
Holding back.

We were
Conversing
Till night's
Early dawn,
When we
Both realized
I was still
Holding her
Strong.

Changing breeze
Her shoulder
Goose bumps
Put on,
That's when
I kissed her
And sang
A sweet song.

We arose,
And accepted
Gratefully
Sun's warming
Rays,
I told her
I would
Love her
The rest
Of my days.

She looked
At me open
And saw
I really am
A beautiful
Loving
Ageless
Old man.

I stepped
Back into
My watery
Home,
Saying if she
But need
Send a note
On a leaf
And to her
I would come.

She put
Her hands
To her face
I said to
Be brave,
To rebuild
Her life
And be
No one's
Slave.

Spring
Summer
Or Fall
At your
Beckon call;
What about
Winter
She said.

It's true
I live life
In and out
Of the deep
But Winter's
Reserved
For other
Promises
Keep.

I waved
My hand
And
Blew her
A kiss
Told her
To go back
Before
She was
Missed.

She smiled
Then strength
And color
Returned,
A suicide note
From memory
She burned.

With only
One eye
Above
Watery
Bay,
I watched
Her turn smiling
And walk
Slowly away.

The sun
Was now up
Moon and stars
Gave way
To daytime's
Awakening
And Creations
Full sway.

Light hearted
I floated
Barely submerged,
Knowing sadness
Stalked Spirit
Again
Had been
Purged.

Lazy current
I'm riding
Turns round
The bend,
Open heart
Broadcasts,
Receives
And does
Send.

Out here again
In the open
Quite far
From the
Shore,
Sunburn threatens
My life
Stinging
My pores.

So down
To the bottom
I dive
The deep
All's quiet
Inside
As wind goes
To sleep.

Check in
With spirit
Why do I leave
Seems too long
A time
Since blessing
Received.

Within cosmic
Glow
Promise to stay,
I know I'm
Here drifting,
Far far away.

After what seems
Like eternity,
I open my eyes
But it's too dark
To see.

There's
Something here
Tickling
My knee
It's Tuggy
The Dugong
Befriending me.

He and I
Go back
To when
We were
Pups,
Same Mother
We share
Downs with
The ups.

Tuggy and Maia
Long have
Had kids
Of their own,
Two generations
The coop
Have they flown.

New family
And friends
Crowd around
Wishing me
Well,
They all
Have fantastic
Stories to tell.

But Tuggy says
It's up to
The surface
With you,
Though you're
Safe with us
Here
Your body's
Quite blue.

Humans
Look funny
I hear a
Little one say,

Here comes
The surface,
Nephews and nieces
Already at play.

The whole clan
Is here shouting
Hip-hip hooray,
Wanting to know
If I'm back
Now to stay.

Just a spin
Around town
I'm out on a lark,
That's when
I notice
It's beginning
To get dark.

Come with us then
At least
Part of the way,
For we are
Migrating
To Hummingbird
Cay.

The kids
Grab my fingers
The teeners
Push me along,
Guess that
I'm going
Desire's
Too strong.

Swimming
With mother
We yield
To her flow,
Sun sets
The evening
Stars start
Their show.

It's a beautiful
Night
Animal symphony
Galore,
Bullfrogs
Keep rhythm
On far reedy
Shore.

Mother's current
Highlights
A low rolling
Swell,
While far off
Lights twinkle
Near ships
Channel bell.

Heady with
Life's music
We paddle along,
Amazed at the
Intimate newness
Of Mother's
Sweet song.

None of us here
Fear it won't Last

We live in
The moment
Forgotten
The past.

Been here
For days
Lost track of
Time clockings Sun,
Like what I do
We're all having
Fun.

Throughout
The night
My kin
Laugh and play,
For they all
Know
You stay
Healthy
That way.

Tug and Maia
Swim up close
To my side,
Asking politely
I'm tired,
Would I
Like a ride?

Rolling over
On my back
With a grin
And a sigh,
Each offers
A flipper,

They're
Much more
Buoyant
Than I.

With both
Of them there
I close
Tired eyes,
Maia is singing
Her best lullaby.

Soon me
Their cargo
Is fast asleep,
Dreaming
Adventures
In vast
Briny deep.

Tuggy's there
With me
My very
Best friend,
Living our
Moments
Seen without
End.

Briny deep
Is Mother unknown,
That's where
Seeds of order
From chaos
Are regully
Sewn.

Chaos
From order
Is part
Of it too,
The heart
In its
Wisdom
Knows
Just what
To do.

We see
It all clearly
With Loves
Inner eye,
We are
The cosmos,
Watching
Dugongs
Swim by.

Grandmother
Uma
Glides up
With the
Dawn,
Pointing out
Shoreward
Innocent fawn.

We are in
Backwater
Channel
It leads to
Hummingbird
Cay,
Blinking my eyes
We've come
A long way.

Morning birds
Give praise
To round
Setting moon,
Showing me
Berries on boughs,
Won't need a spoon.

There's plenty of
Hyacinth and
Some kind of cress,
Dugongs are choosey
But don't
Leave a mess.

Catfish cousins
Wonder
What kind of
Critter I be,
All covered
With hair,
They've
Never seen
A fish
Look like me.

We all
Have a laugh
At Catfish
Expense,
That's when
I remember
I'm not
Wearing pants.

My skin is
All wrinkled

Dirt draws
A blank,
My feet
Haul me out
On opposite
Bank.

Mud between toes
Feels squishy
And cool
Cocklebur comb
Is a mighty
Fine tool.

Legs are like
Rubber
Not used to
Gravity's weight,
Sit in
Dry leaves
Facing sunrise,
I meditate.

The family fed
Moves on
Down the line,
Tuggy swims by
His heart
Touching mine.

We never goodbye
But say
See ya soon,
Perhaps when
The cycle
Makes another
Full moon.

I sit there
Connected
Sun warms
My skin,
The smell
Of home cooking
Comes wafting in.

Overhearing
Small voices
The air they
Excite,
They've spied
A stranger
In the clearing,
He doesn't
Look right.

Fatherly sounds
Acknowledge
Their plight,
Footfalls
Are heard
But they are
Quite light.

Standing before me
He thinks
I am daft,
Wanting
To know
Where is
My raft.

I tell him
I swam here
With Dugong
Family,

Spent the night
Dreaming
In bottomless
Sea.

He calls
Out to Ma
To please
Bring him
Some clothes,
I show him
Webs between
Fingers
Skin plugs
Keep water,
Out of my nose.

He wants
To know
If I intend
Harm,
They only
Have children
And a very small
Farm.

No harm
Will come
From this
Respecter of life,
Not even a hand
Put on his
Hard working wife.

Come up
To eat at

Our house then
Though the
Money's
All spent,
I see by
Their demeanor
They're quite
Tolerant.

Sitting at the table
The home has
One room,
I feel happiness
And laughter
Absence
Of gloom.

My eyes
Catch the grain
Of the worn
Wooden floor
As Grandfather
Enters through
A back door.

His eyes
Sparkle
Dancing
He saw me
At dawn,
We were
Both watching
The very
Same fawn.

This is he
Who swims
With
Dugong

Down to the Sea,
Welcome my Son
You're in good
Company.

Children all
Watchful
At windows
And doors,
He calls
Them in
They've finished
With chores.

I meet their eyes
With a smile
And a grin,
With open heart
I welcome them In.

The oldest
Steps forward
And holds
Out his hand,
Saying
Welcome to
Our house
Our hearts
And our
Land.

I thank him
His grace
With web
Fingered
Hand
He isn't afraid
As before me
He stands.

His sisters
And brothers
All crowd
Around,
Wanting
To know
If Dugongs
Make sounds.

I laugh
With a nod
Singing Maia's
Melody,
The same one
Last night
She sang
For me.

I see the youngest
Peering from
Behind Mother's
Long dress,
Beckon her over
To join
With the rest.

She is quite shy
Red cheeked Cherub
This life,
She has
The beautiful eyes
Of the farmers
Fair wife.

She runs
To her Father

Who sits
By my side,
Covers her face
With his hand
The child
Is his pride.

He lifts her up
To sit
In his lap,
She wants to know
Does my mom
Make me
Take naps.

We laugh
All around
Breakfast
Is served,
Children
Put plates
Out
Gone is
Reserve.

There is
Oatmeal
Toast
And brown egg,
Goat's milk
Cheese
And a
Hound dog
To beg.

After a prayer
We all dig in,

Passing
The toast
The chewing
Begins.

I see the good
Here
Lives full
Of Love,
Everyone's
Happy
God's Light
Is inside,
Not just above.

I help with the Dishes
The children
Put them away
I give each
A gold Hyacinth
On their way
Out to play.

For the Mother
I have a
Gold inlaid
Turtle shell Comb,
I know it has
Finally, found
A good home.

To Grandfather
Cheerful
I give a new pipe
A little tobacco
The kind
That he likes.

The Father
On bended knee
Do I Knight,
For long
Faithful
Service
And loving
His wife.

Out in the
Sunlight
I bless
Their
Small farm,
Asking God
To protect them
From future
Storm harm.

From the gate
I turn
And they wave,
Removing
The clothing
I place
In each
Pocket
A golden
Doubloon,
Found where
Storms rave.

It is a
Spectacular
Morning
The path
Parallels
The slough,

It's exactly
The direction
I'm wanting
To go.

The leaves
Overhead
Shade speckle
The trail,
I'm with
The unknown
Loves in
My heart,
You know
I can't fail.

My life
Is become easy
Much less
Difficult,
I still intend
Desires
And wishes,
But gave up
Owning
Results.

Thank
Lucky stars
Even by day,
I'm now
Living life
In a most
Colorful way.

Even abroad
I'm still
Here at home,
Thankful
To learn
The meaning
Of Aum.

Walk
Run
And swim
Happily
Throughout
The day
By myself
All
The while
Yet never
Alone,
I've rounded
The corner
And headed
For home.

Up on a hill
Known as
Blue Ridge,
I see
Mother River
Below
Flowing under
Old bridge.

# Marimba

ovely
Marimba,
Patiently
I await
Your birth.
Daughter
Pearl
Says that
Shall be
Your name
When you
Arrive.
I can
See it all
Now.
Awakening
Boisterously
You proclaim
Your
Birthright
And with
Strength
Known only
To the newborn
Will you
Accept your
Time
Among us.
Gratefully
Shall I hold

You
In my arms
While your
Mother
Catches
Her breath.
We shall
Lovingly
Bond together
Forever
Recognizing
We are
All along
Old soul mates;
Perhaps once
Even I
Was your
Child.
Just knowing
You exist
Puts strength
Back into
My arm,
Resolve returns
Like
The swallows
Eager
To build
Their nests
And bear
Their young.
A special
Excited
Frenzy
Fills
My heart,

It is
Joy
Revealed
Unto
The world.
I shall
Be known,
As grandfather.
Did I
Mention
How wonderful
It felt
To hold
Your mom
When
She was
Born?
It was a time
Of all times
Watching
Life
Enter her
Tiny body.
She looked
Around,
Her eyes
Knew God.

# Phenomenon Stone

n the early
Morning skies
Sol rises
And begins
To clear away
The fog.
It has rained
Softly
Off and on
The night
Before
And the ground
Is quite
Saturated.
Small shallow
Puddles
Lie in wait
For their
Own personal
Reflections –
Quietly
Expectant
Of a new found
Face
Illumined
By the young
Bright Sun.
On the patio
Of the abandoned
Main house,

The grey man
Officiates
Expectantly
At the birthing
Of new green
Shoots;
Pearl's daffodils,
Hyacinth
And tulips.
He finds
The neatly
Planted
Exhibition
Exhilarating.

Silently
He glides
Across
The flagstones
Leading through
The gardens,
His new
Insulated boots
Disdainful
Of the cold mud.
Out
In the orchard,
He finds
The buds
Still sleeping.
January
Is deep
In winter now
And the trees
Are resting.
Year after year

He tends them
Whether they
Bear fruit
Or not.
In his solitude
He shares
His soul
With the trees,
Pruning
Watering
And feeding;
Ever watchful
For parasite
And insect,
Removing them
And asking
Forgiveness
In taking
Their life.
The old grey man
Loves
The trees
With all
His heart
And continues
To remain
Among them
Even when
All else fails.
The wild
Migrating birds
Have learned
To tolerate him
For they see
He means
No harm

And willingly
Shares the fruit
With all
Who come around.
In return,
The birds help
With infestations
And nest
Their young
Within the safety
Of the branches.
The snows
Are light
Here in this
Part of
The high desert
Laying close to
The Mogollon rim.
And the trees
Take to his
Nurturing.
Even the
Specimen
And windbreak
Evergreens
Grow in
Exuberance,
Old enough now
To produce
Seed
And young
Of their own.

The air
Is cool
And clean,

The fragrance
Of wet
Red-brown
Earth
Is carried gently
Upon the
Slightest breeze.
All is well.
The grape starts,
Three to
A bucket,
Sing of
Coming life,
The nearing
Dance of Spring.
Even the shouts
Of school children
In the yard
Down the road
Blend with
A bright blue
Puffy cloud
Sky.
All is well
And yet,
Old Grey
Is dissatisfied,
Unfinished
With himself.
He feels,
Incomplete.
A gnawing
Emptiness
That won't
Leave;
A feeling

Of unfinished
Business
Between himself
And his maker.

At different times
In his life
Grey spied
The Truth
From the corners
Of his eyes
While sitting
Quietly
In the wilderness.
This intimacy
Frightened him
For he felt
To be
The intruder
Upon such
A great
And peaceful
Intelligence.
For years
He thought
On this,
Wishing
To be accepted
By whatever
It is that waits
And is always
Ready
To be known.
Today,
Grey understood
The opportunity

Is within.
It happened
Among
The newly planted
Seedling junipers,
Close hid
Under the brush
On the low hill
Behind his small
Shack.
The rain soaked
Lichen covered
Rocks
Seemed to glisten
A new radiance
In recognition.

The hill entire
Came alive
To a silent
Song.
Small birds
Rise up to branch,
Clamoring
And reassure
The fresh eye
All is happening
As IT IS
Wont to do.
Denying
A hastily
Concocted fear
Grey steps
Forward.
The door
To a dead past

Closes silently
Behind
For there are none
To hear.
Internal therapy
Triumphant
At last,
He sees
The story
Of last night's
Dream
To be
A true tale
Of the path;
And even though
He walks alone
Grey knows
In his heart
All are on
the journey
Together.
With this,
The blue
Of the sky
Returns
To his eyes
And he feels
Somehow,
Younger.

<u>II</u>
Coming back
To himself,
He finds
His person
Sitting upon

A short
Squared stone
Near the brow
Of the low hill.
It is now
Early afternoon
And he wonders
Where
The morning
Went.
Recalling now,
A journey
Within himself
Yet outside.
Somehow
All around.
Remembering
Again
The universe
Uncontained
Is also inside
Of himself
Expanding
With each breath
Exploding into
Untold galaxies
Without end
Yet touchable
Even unto
The most
Insignificant
Molecule.
Here,
The most
Extravagant
Activity

Is found to be
In league with
The ultimate
Silence,
And in the
Ensuing
Stillness
He sees we are
Each
Uniquely
Similar.
His God
Is your
God
Is.
The Mother
Of all natures
Comforts him
Enfolding
With arms
Everlasting
The small
Inner child
Who has tumbled
Out of
The self-imposed
Prison,
Blinded
Temporarily
By the light.
The magnitude
Of being aware
Is augmented
By the old dog
As she nuzzles
The palm of

Her master's hand
While he realizes
All along
Bess knows
The truth
And has been
Laying there
Beside him
Keeping watch.
The abundance
Of a melting
Heart
Rises like
A bird's wing
Cacophony
Revealing
Once
And for all,
It is
Love
At the helm
Of this,
Our universe.
Love is
The ultimate
Power
For it leads
The way,
Follows after,
And is the nest
We frontier.
Within,
Around
And through,
We are
Surrounded

By this
One love.
Constantly
Protected
We are
Even allowed
To think we can
Harm ourselves
In order to find
The way.
The younger Grey
Opens his misty eyes
To view a small
Brown striped
Lizard
With a bright
Blue tail
Couched
Upon his knee.
It is this
Little one
Who is speaking
Truth
Profound.

This little one
Who could
Be sleeping
Dormant
Deep in the
Cool damp sand
Is gazing up
At Grey,
Heart to heart,
Offering
A secret seed

Held tight
In outstretched
Tiny hand.
Plant
This knowing
In your soul
Keep it safe
At night,
And if you
Are able
To love
Enough,
You will
Become
The light.
Nothing less than
Transfiguration
Full and complete,
Is in store
For those
Who choose not,
The path
Of darkened sleep.
Rather,
Strive for
The real
Truth
Found within
Your
Inner knowing
Unique,
And you
Will become
Both yourself,
And what
It is

You seek.
The flow of man
Is but a trickle
Now
In the face
Of chaos
Dark with doom,
But favor
The Light
With your
Numbers great
And wilt the
Darkest bloom.
For nothing less
Than true relief
Is in store
For those
Whose journey
Is complete,
For once again
You'll reside
Within
Creator's Heart,
And not at
Some tyrant's feet.
Emancipate
Yourself
By freeing
Your Self
Of fear's
Choking clutch,
And hold
Your head high
Give away
Your love,
Accepting

God's own
Perfect touch.
Yes,
This is
The greatest
Time
The turning
Point
Of man.
Of all the
Impossible
Tasks
You breech,
This is one
You can.
A great day
Of reckoning
For all
This life
Did you embark,
It's up to you
To top it all
And honorably
Leave your
Mark.
Even bugs
Have ears
And know
The truth
Of this
Mother's Earth
Upon which
They crawl
Swim fly
And walk,
And soon enough

It will be
Their turn
To try and toe
The mark.
And all
The creatures
Large and small
Shall someday
Pass by
In review,
And all they be
Is recompense
For the legacy
Left by you.
Now you know
We are one
No harm
We do
Each other,
That little bird
Who spoke up
Years ago
To cheer you on
Is my older
Brother.
Remember now
That special
Brother tree
In the forest
That sang
Our song;
Loves you still
And always will
You've been
Gone today
So long.

Come away
With your
Self
That center within
You found,
And accept
Your destiny
Of light
Where you become
The one of might
Upon whom
Love is crowned.

III
The child's
Blue eyes
Slowly open
To find
Sol
Setting down.
The air
Is grown chill,
Little One
Is long gone
And old Bess
Stirs
Raising
Her head;
A question
To go home
In her eyes
Yet a knowing
There is
No hurry
Here.

# Little Wheels

weet Love,
You fill
My heart
My soul
My days
My eyes,
Your being
Brings
Life to me
Your wonder
Fills
The skies.
I cannot
Go far
Enough
With words
Of trust
Or deed;
Or story
Wide enough,
To span
Your birthing
Seed.
I look
To you for
Healing balm
To soothe
Hurts
Deep inside,
And gladly

Give you
Away again
There's
No end
To life's
Ebb tide.
I've just
Found out
There is
No end
To you
The engine
Of this train,
And you
Go everywhere
And can
Be found,
Even in
The rain.

The sun
Again
Goes down
Behind
Clouds of
Scarlet red,
I take
Comfort
You reside
Within
My heart,
And not
Just in
My head.
It is
Nighttime

Now
The breeze
Sleeps
In the trees
With many
A tired bird,
The cricket
Sings
By rubbing
Wings
And Mother
Keeps
Her word.
With
Waning moon
I'll keep vigil
This long
Industrious
Night,
For prayers
Are working
Hard
To mend
All human
Souls,
And bring us
To the
Light.
With love
Set free
Beyond the
Mental fence
Of our
Daily locks
And frowns,
We can

Cut loose
Our fetters
Tight
And don
Our caps
And gowns.
With freedom's
Threshold
Beneath
My feet
And courage
At my side,
I shall keep
Forever more
Wisdom
As my guide.
For years
I felt
My fear
And was
Terrified
Of the dark,
Until it too
Gave up
Its ghost
The light
Has left
Its mark.
I now
Proudly join
All kindred
Souls
In the
Great song
That is our life,
And wed

Love itself
My best friend
Precious
Loving wife.
Into this
Loving
Blinding light
Do I enter
Willingly,
No shadow
Threat
Or endeavor
Dark
Shall ever
Dare
Touch me.
For in
The light
Of His
Truth
No secret
Remains
Concealed,
And sooner
Than later
Confusion's
Source
Will hereby
Be revealed.
Why
From home
We ran
Away
To forget
God
Doesn't matter,

What's
Important
Now
Is finding
Love's
Pathway home,
To a loving
Celestial
Father.

This time
In between
Is filled
With Trial
And strife
Full of
Tribulation,
Our dream
Now comes
Together fast
As one big
Illumined
Nation.
I've seen
The works
Of those
Who labor
Quietly
Behind
The scene,
Their aid
Is the
Grace
That covers
Me
And keeps my

Conscience clean.
Perpetual motion
Is this love
But it's not
Some kind
Machine,
It's made
Of countless
Moving parts
Our heart's
Domain
Its fling.

Even the air
Is charged
With flair
This regal one's
Abroad,
And all
Us little
Wheels
Become
Big deals
When joined
In brotherhood.
It is
Coming soon
When mountains
Shake
Clouds grow
Dark
And oceans
Toss
Their waves,
Love enough
Our concert

Make
And many
Will be
Saved.
The answer
Is found
Inside ourselves
Let's join in
Hand to hand,
And with
Our Love
Go round 'n round,
Make this
The promised
Land.

# Take Wing

ittle bird,
Whose tiny tracks
Barely sign
The gossamer
Of early
Frost,
Your family flits
Across the yard
A hunt
For seeds
Among the twigs
Till only husks
Are lost.
You appear
So small
And weak
Your strength
Is family tie,
And with
A warning beak
You all
Take up,
And fly.
Yet return again
To cold hard
Winter ground
A frugal feast
To share,
And even sentries
Have their turn

---

While others
Are aware.
With my tiny bag
Of store-bought
Seed
All gone
I offer the last
Of bread,
And bid you
Sleep safe
This night
Within your
Bowery bed.
Your songs
Of conquest
And travels broad
Through
Canyon wide
And over
Mountain spire,
Fill me
With wonder
For your kind,
My heart
Will never tire.
The conversation
Between yourselves
Covers life's
Wide range,
I love to
Come around
And listen in
Even though
You think
I'm strange.
Over the years

I've learned
So much
From you
First hand
This big
Wide world,
It's as though
I know
Her secrets too
Like how
Trees roots
Are burled.
And also
How mountains
Get so tall
And why
Rivers run
So deep,
 – And why
It is
The glaciers cold
Never seem
To sleep.
 – And why
The moon
So full turns
An ebbing
Tide,
 – And why
Love keeps
A precious mate
Forever
By your side.
 – And why
Too much
Curiosity

Can sometimes
Bring regret,
And why
Waves
Roll up
The beach
The sand's
Already wet.
– And why
Clouds
Are really
Drops of rain
Borrowed
From shining sea,
Just like
The countless
Souls
From beyond
All time,
Born to learn
To be.
– And why
Does one
Have so many
Lives
Scattered beyond
All sight,
Is because
I'll keep
Coming back
Until I get it right.
– And why
There is no
Need to fear
Or pace the path
In hurry,

No one
Is ignored
By God,
Or forgot
In eon's
Flurry.
And that
Is why we take
The time
To make
Good friends
That last,
'Cause here we are
Among ourselves
Making now
Our future
Past.
And even though
A freshly
Furrowed field
May appear
To be aught
But stone
And soil,
It is really
Brought
About
By Mother Earth,
Son and
Creator's toil.
Look now
Between the rows
For seed
Grub and worm,
And like the bird
You too will find

There is
Much here
You can learn.
The seeds of joy
Planted
In my heart
Makes
For early
Perpetual
Spring,
And that
Is why
My life
In all its glory
Gladly
Takes to wing.

# One Day's Glory

itting quietly
Amid gloaming
Sunbeams
Of our
Setting sun
One has
Chance
To relax
And reflect
Upon
The happenings
Of this day.

Like the
Temperate
Breeze
That kicks up
And takes
Notice of this
Celestial
Changing
Of the guard,
The mind
Swirls around
The day's
Activities
Like the
Streaming
Clouds
Caught

In a quickly
Darkening sky.
Soon the stars
Will be out
In record
Number
As the
Recent rain
Has cleared
The valley
Air of dust
And soot
Cast up
By the denizen's
Mutual decree.

Dahlsen agreed
Early on
This afternoon,
Today is indeed
A glorious
Winter's day.

The girls
Were being
Angels
As usual
Making it
Easy
To say yes
To their
Every whim.

Desires
Were met
Easily

Today
Not just
Because
Nothing
Difficult
Occurred,
Rather
A positive
Acceptance
Of what
Is,
Smoothed
Over the
Rough spots
Preventing
Ruffles
And feathers
From
Getting together.

Actually
Some could say
There is
Good reason
To be upset;
I've no
Steady job
And there
Is but
Thirty-eight cents
In the house
And a whopping
Forty-one cents
In the bank
At last count.

And yet,
Every need
Was met.
Slivers
Got pulled
And all the
Broken glass
Was harvested
Carefully.

Weeds were
Hauled
Stuff got
Pruned
And the sun
Shone
Warm and friendly.

Even Stryder's
Papers
Of independence
Were notarized.

For a moment
A sharp sadness
Welled up
Behind my eyes
And headed
For my heart
But was
Quickly replaced
By the joy
In knowing
He is all
Grown up now
And on his own.

The statement
Of emancipation
Was the last
Small tie
To yesterday
And my
Little boy.

Suddenly,
It was easy
To let go.

I sealed
The moment
With a
Grateful prayer
And set it free
To sail away
On the current
Of Grace Divine.

He is doing
Well
Just like
I always
Knew he would.

Today,
Saturday,
Was a good
Time to get
Things done
Out in
The yard.

Spring is
Just around
The corner
And it feels
Good to be
Getting on top
Of all the
Garden chores.

It felt
Especially good
To lay down
For a nap
And rest
My tired back.

A flute
Was playing
Softly
On the set
And as I
Looked across
The room
My eyes
Fell upon
The new bicycle
Parked
In front of
The desk.
Just like
A kid
You bet
I keep it
In the house.

Mud and all.

Forty-five minutes
Of the best
Sleep
I've had
In days
Left me
Refreshed
And as I
Opened
My eyes
I became aware
That all
The aches
And dizziness
Had passed.

Laying there
Among the
Last notes
Of that beautiful
Music
I realized
Just how
Blessed
We really are.

I have found
My God.

The search
Is over.

# Yoke With No Tether

ere
In all
The turmoil
Stirred
By Love
One often
Stops
To clear
The air
Knowing
Heart is
Always right.

Sometimes
It takes only
A lifetime
To really
See it all
And actually
Clear
The sight.

We each
Have this thing
Called
Eternity,
A compendium
Of all
There is
In which

To fit
Our story's
Lore
And bear witness
To our
Light.

It doesn't
Matter
How long
It takes
Except to
Fear's
Imagined loss,
And even
In confusion's
Mountain wake
Objective
Wrong or right,
I remember
Heart's logic
Surreal
And 'bide
In Love's
Great might.

Love never
Takes
It only
Gives
And forever
Will it wait
Till I
Come 'round
Again;
In this

Love is
Delight.

The quiet cat
A calling bird
The still
Cool air
In my room
At night
All know
Love's truth
And winning
Ways
Are watchful
Like a
Barking dog's
Howling
Moon
A crescent
Of what
Is to come,
A promise
Shining
Bright.

I find
Difficulty
Only within
Myself
Monkeys
In the dark,
A kindly
Person
Took time
To draw
The curtain

Back
And held up
The lantern
Bright.

I was not
Alone
It felt
Good
To see
The others
Share relief,
We all
Took time
To love
Those parts
Left undone
By hurry's
Yesterday,
And the newness
Of a knowing
Vibe
Swelled
Our gladness
With
Moving
Hearts
Deep into
The night.

The songs
We sang
Were new
To us
Yet old
As time
Itself,
No matter

Where
We went
With consciousness
We found
Ourselves
In light.

And then
It happened
All at once
An explosion
Of sound
And might,
Our universal
Claxon call
Caught
Fire,
Lit up the darkest
Night.

Throughout
The galaxy
A starry glow
Sprang up
Like fireflies
Of a balmy
Summer's eve,
The idea
Caught
On
A wildfire
Pace
And spread
Across
The cosmic
Stage

From yesterday
To tomorrow's
Promise,
Then flew on
Out of
Sight.

And here
We are
The breath
In one
Movement
Echos
The still,
And sweet dreams
Our lives
Become,
The burden
Is all right.

There is
No need
To search
For truth
Or seek
Perfection
Anymore,
We're already
Perfect
In God's eyes
So let's get on
With what
We are
Here to do,
Serve each other
With delight.

# Tooth And Nail

usic's
Spineret
Weaves
A story
We call
Home
Our hearts
An open
Door;
A welcome
To all
Who enter
Here,
And countless
Feet
Polish bright,
The ancient
Flagstone floor.

The dust
Of centuries
Blows away
In a moments
Wily gust,
The Truth
Uncovered
Gives
A wink
And life
Divests
Its trust.

The early
Dawn
Spots
The newest
Forms
Of destiny
Manifest,
The countryside
Which is
Our nature pure,
Is now
Truly blessed.

A people
Diverse
Who were
Tagged
With a caring
Charge
And at once
Had lagged
Behind,
Find new
Hope within
Each other's
Truth
And follow
Favored sign.

Safe within
The higher Self
Which has
Waited patient
All this
Time,
We come

To terms
With all
Our games
And filter
Out the
Bind.

This
Inner Self
Connect
With God
Our one way
Ticket home,
Forever waving
At the gate,
In silence
Fights for us,
Tooth
And nail
And stone.

# Chance Upon

he night
That honors
Smiles
On us
Here below
In quiet's
Arms
I find
Myself
Renewed
Once more
Beguiled
By mystery's
Charms.

And all
This errant
Wonderland
Is mingled
With town
And backward
Time,
So that
Wilderness
Is doorbell's
Ring
And all
That's God
Is mine.

For what
Is love,
But a bed
Of friendly

Leaves
To rest
A broken
Heart;
A constant
Friend
That begins
Again
To make
Another
Start.

So don't
Forget
To bless
The clouds
With a
Nearby place
To go,
For what
Is a
Mountain peak
Without
Its share
Of snow.

A chance
Upon
A labor's
Love
Is life's
Work
Moon to sun,
And when
Found
What I
Came here
Most to do
Is when
I will
Be done.

# Love Understands

rops
Of gathered
Rain fall
From sleeping
Apple branch
Wind
Slows down
To gentle
Breeze
Green boughs
Comb the air,
We're warm
Inside my love
And I
Snug at home,
In our
Easy chair.

A breakfast
Full of light
Music
Everywhere,
Raindrops
Falling
On the roof
From one
Big cloud
Of blueless
Sky,
A silence
Uncompare.

I told her
That I
Love her
Round eyes
Gave me
Away
To joy
Born from
Within;
Fear of loss
It overwhelmed,
With flowers
Everywhere
My life
Can
Now begin.

We think
Each other's
Thoughts
The raindrops
Our
Everyday,
Flow together
In passion's
Flood
I am a
Thief
She say.
I stole
Her heart
In a
Mountain
Storm;
I tell her
It is safe

With me and tree,
And though
It is forever
Lost to her,
It will never
Cease
To be.

Unattached
Is more than
Good enough
For the likes
Of me;
She looks
Deep within
My soul
And sets
My spirit
Free.
We decide
To drown
The universe
With love,
The kind
Felt by
She and me,
The good news
Is that it's
Already full,
A gift from
(The busy)
Honey bee.

She looks
At me
From across

The room
I can feel
Shivers
Down
Her spine,
The sparkle
In my eyes
Responds
To her
Loving touch
A tiny
Mountain's
Waterfall,
Her hand
It touches
Mine.

I bless her
When she
Sneeze
I bless her
In her
Sleep,
I pray
To God
Please
Heal her
Pain
Our love
Is running
Deep.

The gentle
Rain
Cools
The air

And stiffens
Up
The breeze,
Raindrops
Try and
Turn
To snow
Wild birds
Hide
In trees.

Now
The rain
Turns
To snow
Falls silent
To hungry
Ground,
A romance
Continues
On in
Love
So old
It's always
New,
And is
Welcome
Found.

The flurries
Fall
But do not
Stick
The ground
Is warm
Snowflake

Turns
To rain,
Its patter
Upon
Our little
Roof
Keeps rhythm
With the flame.

The breeze
Steps up
To wind
And blows
The trees
Around,
Early on
I spread
Birdseed
On the path
And gave
A happy shout!
Their breakfast
Has been found.

From flake
To rain
Rain and rain
And back
To flake again,
The morning's
Filled
With
Simple chores
The billy
Boils refrain.

The rain
It stops at noon
I guess
To catch its breath,
Then continues on
At 12 0 5
To what
Appears,
A certain
Muddy death.

But wait,
Each drop
Is just
Transformed
By
Drooping leaf
And quiet
Thirsty root,
The droplets
Have not died
Or gone away
They've become
Instead
New shoots.

Much the same
As I
When learned
I'm not
This body
Get,
A simple
Shift
Love understands,
All else
Illusions
Wet.

# In The Garden

 fter the storm
Snow here
Melts fast

Spring
Is in
A hurry
To bloom

Last
Of the old
Weeds
Give up
Their ground
Begrudgingly

Winter's
Bird
Rakes stubble
In the pasture
Searching
For remnants
Of last year's
Bounty

Not too many
Flowers
Can be found

---

Locally
Just yet
But if one
Looks closely
A few Periwinkle
Fleabane
And purple Iris
Can be seen
Daring to display
Their wares

The crispness
Of the air
Is warmed
Tentatively
By a fresh
Yellow sun
Blocked
Temporarily
By receding
Storm clouds
Their work
Hereabouts
Finished
For now

The blue
Of the skies
Washed clean
By rain and snow
Is almost harsh
In its strident
Clash
With Winter's
Hold upon
The land

I can hear
The neighbor's
Truck
Struggle
To the
Rutted mud
Reserved
For the
Brown
Winding track

Being low
Here
In this part
Of  the valley
The snow
Melts easily
To the tune
Of meltwater's
Promise
And exposes
Rich brown
Earth
Strewn with
Limestone
Pebbles
And other
Fragments
Opalized
By time
Already ancient
When other
Beings
Layed claim
To these
Terraces

That were
Once floors
Of inland
Seas

How timeless
It all seems
As I stand
Here
With pitchfork
And rake
Gazing down
At the
Muddy soil
Realizing
My own place
In eternity
While smelling
The pungent
Odor
Of rotted
Compost
As it surrenders
Nutrient
To the ground

With a firm
Inner knowing
I recognize
This long train
Of many lives
Is slowing down
To the dull
Roar
Of a thousand
Waterfalls

Perhaps
Not too
Many more
Trips
Will I make
Before
The station
Of illumination
Arrives

It is inevitable
Such a thing
Will come
To pass

Even when
I began
The journey
The feeling
Of completion
Was there
In the back
Of my heart

And now
The growing
Certainty
Produced
By careful
Self realization
Compounds
The excitable
Pulse
Of running
Feet
In this life's
Anticipation

I gaze upon
A small flock
Of winter
Sparrows
As they
Take up
To barren
Branch
From
Chilly ground
At the edge
Of my plot

They all look
Back at me

I can tell
They know
I'm the one
Who puts
Seed out
For them

They are
Not afraid
Or in a
Hurry
For possibly
More easy seeds
Will get tossed
Around
To feast on

The sun
Is getting
Ready

To pass
Behind
Winter's
Southern
Frozen mountain
Signaling me
To end
Another day
Of preparation
For Spring

Turning slowly
With  tools
Slung
Over my
Shoulder
I leave
The silent
Rows
To my feathered
Friends

I know
They will
Tend their
Garden well
Just as
Their ancestors
Did
Before me.

# Gift Of Life

The older gentleman
Whose hair is slowly
Turning white
Looks down at his lap
Gazing upon
A newborn granddaughter.
Some of the wrinkles
Are missing
From his weatherbeaten face.
He has never been
Too good at giving,
But by receiving her
Into his heart
He is learning how.
The glow emanating
From his eyes
As he lovingly
Gazes upon her
Is returned immediately
By the tiny infant
Whose own dark eyes
Spark a quiet clarity
Already ancient
In the wisdom
Of the moment.
The old tabby
Sits beside his leg
Leaning up against
His worn trowsers
Rubbing her jaw

Into his shin.
She is also here
To bask in the glory
Of all that life
Has to offer.
She shows no interest
In the small young mouse
Brazenly exposed now
From behind her very own
Stuffed toy
In the far corner
Of the sunlit room.
As the baby
Finds its small mouth
With a tiny plump fist
The young mother
Smiles down upon her also.
She is standing
On the grandfather's left
With her delicate hand
Resting upon his shoulder.
The infant kicks
At the little blanket
Covering her legs
And smiles back
At them both.
Just then,
A small quiet breeze
Runs through
The wind chimes
Out on the narrow porch
Authoring
A knowing look
Between father
And daughter.
Heartfelt excitement

Rises unrestrained
For they both know
Some of the guardian angels
Have come forth
To see the child.
The golden sunlight
Grows brighter
In that small room
And the canary
Shifting slightly
On its perch,
Begins to sing.
Some of the birds outside
Answer, and immediately
Fly off to spread the news.
A tiny inchworm
Who has spent
The entire morning climbing
Up to the open window,
Now stands upon the sill
Stretching as far as possible
Into the room
The better to get
A good look.
Curiosity is not
A trait of his.
He has come
To give his blessing.
With short jerky bows
He now casts
Holy water
Into the room
From a tiny golden
Cross-encrusted bowl,
Too small to be seen.

The tiny ants
Who have been pirating
Bread crumbs
Left on the sill
For the outside birds
Even stop.
They turn about
As one unit
And become at once
The papal congregation,
Whispering amongst themselves
At how beautiful
She is.
Even though the people
In that small house
Are poor
And no one in particular,
There is no denying
The fact that life
Wherever it is found
Is a truly, sacred gift.

# First Chair

eep in the damp
Of caverns huge,
Torchlight stars
The ancient walls
Of heaven.

A wedge of moon
In crescent rise
Beyond the gaping mouth
To outside death,
Chases wayward children
Into the womb
Of  Mother in her night.

II
Shaman helpers
Spark the fire
Dry grasses smoulder
Hot new life,
And chills run risk
Of many eyes
Caused by rasping dirge
In throaty sound;
The jungle's always right.

Elder shadows
Trace their tale
On inky walls
And gyre for fallen friends
Fabled battles lost and won.

Layed in quiet's tomb
Sleeping now
In Mother's arms,
Their broken spears
Placed one last time
In daring hands
Under sprinkle charm
Of ochre gold
And flowered weave
Fragrant sprig of pine.

With tears now dry
Their women place
A journey's meal
Near matted hair
Alongside favored tools
And ivory fetish bright.
Covered in last goodby
By bloody soil
Where song lives on
Of killer beast,
The fallen eyes are closed
For ever more
To all except
Rebirth's end complete.

<u>III</u>
Darkness shrinks
From common sense
As weathered hands
Throb with drums
And learn'ed feet
Shake up the dust
On soft cool earthen floor.

A couple nose;
A child held tight
In loving arms
Looks out at family tie,
And knows deep within
Its tiny heart
The spark lives on
Spirit rides
Through the rock
And walks
A snakey line.

Tatooed soot
Layed carefully in
One's animal that protects,
Gives surety
To one and all.

Life goes on
As sharpened flint
Of one's own sight
Becomes aware at last,
Of what it is
That comes around
To someday's
Thoughts of now,
And Wisdom's march
In the sea of life.

IV
The survivors learn
More than wait
For illusion's
Often pained regret.

This is progress
Slow yet true,

A deserving move
Toward Light,
A monumental step
Of freedom's gait,
The threshold
Of heaven's touch
A record cast
In someday's stone
My connection
Mountain fast.

We walk away
From fumbling fear
No armored folly
Need I drink
Nor bolstered number
For bravery's feint;
The sunlight
Pouring out within
Brooks no cloud
As life insists
No matter how cramped
A darkened soil.

The brightest of flowers
Grow righteous through
Broken skulls
And shattered bones,
Can I do no less?

V
Cupid's antlered bugle call
On forever's tribal lips;
Arrow's eternal loving bow
Aimed at the heart
Waits only for your founding Truth,
I bless you with a yes!

As ancient worms
Crawl to sleeping flesh
Mothers bare their young
The warriors night
In stars are robed
A staircase is reborn.

Dancers rout
All thought of gloom
Their torsos reverie revealed,
And soon all sorrow
With regret
Leaves hand in broken hand,
No more, to be concealed.

VI
Coming of age
With our Maker sitting in,
Reassures the rain
Of endless leaves,
A bounty,
Manifest.

Magnetic songs
Bless the air we breathe
Torchlight shows the way,
Home is where we always are
Tomorrow
Is our distant hill
Now is a golden tree;
Invisible
Is yesterday fading fast,
In quagmire memory.

VII
With the grinding sound
Of Mother Earth
Roaring in our ears,
Each soul is an orbit
Of the Truth
Our primal chant,
Supreme.

# Rainbow Ride

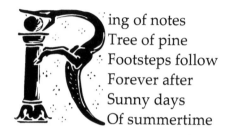ing of notes
Tree of pine
Footsteps follow
Forever after
Sunny days
Of summertime

New flute
To ancient lips divine
Skip along
Together in
Rhythmic playful
Birdsong rhyme

The lifelong wait
Of vision's view
Is a dance of faith
Long on trust
By patience gate
Yet known by few

Only a soulmate
Could possible know
Just what it is
Life's story
Hereby bent
On us bestow

Sunlight somewhere shines
Clouds here lose their rain
A thirsty soil
Soaks up all the tears

Only a summer
Could explain

The wish for freedom
Souls applaud
Found everywhere
Spirit resides
Our world's a stage
Deep with God
Moon's in cycle
With my tides

The quest for Truth
Runs deep in trains
An answer then
As well as now
Is welcome both
By heart and veins

The brain knows where
But heart knows how
Bodies dance
With golden feet
Freedom takes
Another bow

This flute
This tiny reed
Brought forth
In sunny golden throng
Is a farmer well
Who plants the potent seed
Whose sprouted roots
Fill Mother Earth, full in living song

Let hearts connect
With open ears
Receive within

Grace of summer's dove
And go on growing tall
In coming years
Bear the fruit
Of constant love

We evolve
Just like the blue
Allow yourself to give away
All love that comes to you
With a heart so open wide
Life's a rainbow ride so true

All flourish
In this ground of love
Strong lives
Does effort make
Essence crowns
Trials we rise above
Radiant Truth
The path create

I love you true
With blossom heart
My own moon glows
With ebb and flow
To begin again
Is where to start
Bound for home
Is where we go

The trees all wait
For promised rain
The flowers too
Already grown
Thunder growls

In loud refrain
A drop or two
Your very own

O downpour bless
This desert ground
Lightning slash
Please come this way
Fill all the pores
Arid day has found
And quench our thirst
Please come and play

O downpour bless
This desert dry
Sheets of rain
Please come this way
Fill all the pores
Hot days deny
And quench our thirst
Please come and play

O downpour bless
This desert land
Rainbow's arch
Please come this way
Fill all the pores
Arid day has banned
And quench our thirst
Please come and play

# Ocelia

weet love,
Your gentle eyes
Witness the birth
Of my resurrection.

The plaintiff pales
Before the Phoenix
Of an ever wise
Blessing
That rises from
The ashes
Of almost good enough,
Yesterday,
And the flagrant
Immolation
Of sorrow's
Self pity.

Your unflagging Truth
Winnows the chaff
From the grain
Leaving each kernel
Free
Of ignorant
Passiveness,
Free to bask
In the sunlight
Of your willful

Freedom
And clear eyed
Sincerity.

No games
Can be put over
On you.

Only an honest
Silliness
Full of opportune
Candor
Can catch
Your funnybone
Off guard;
The odd view
Of a path
Not taken
Where whimsical
Quips
Still fresh
In their innocence
Lay quietly
Abandoned accidentally,
But not forgotten.

My love,
I look long
Into your honest eyes
And find myself
Reborn
Not a moment
Too soon.

Where and how
I came across

---

Your humble self
Can be reckoned
Only as the path
Which I follow,
The answer
To a heartfelt
Prayer,
A success
Possible only
Because of
Grace.

Your patience
With everyone
Amazes me
Constantly,
And I know truly
Within the quiet place
In my heart,
That it is you
Who is
The real lover
Watching for
The first green shoots;
The ever-faithful hand
That cultivates
Such carefully
Planted seed.

Your Truth
Is the very
Water of life
For I've seen
You save even the weed
And put it to good use.
How do I know this?

I am that very rebel
Who has fallen under
Your irrevocable
Spell
And is eternally
Grateful for discovery
Of the good
You found
Even in one such as I.
My strength
Finds song
In you.

Ocelia, I love you.

Your tenderness
And open display
Of affection
Disarms me,
The calloused outlaw
Who gladly
Remains in the shade
Of your nurturing
Goodness.
I understand now
All of my wanderings
Were only steps
Closer to you.

I can feel
A healing peace
Exponential
In its growth.

Each day,
I am filled with awe

With the wonder
Of awakening glimpses
Into myself,
Which you
So graciously
Provide.

I am happy
To be at your side
And really require
Little else.

I am happy
To share
Your tender moments
And be a witness
As well as
A recipient
Of the good you do
In this world.

Please don't be hard
On yourself
As you have
Taught me
To be more loving
Of who I am.

Thank you
For cherishing
My little child
And always
Being ready
To comfort
And protect.

I have watched you
Learn from me,
From others,
And am continually
Astounded
By your humility
In allowing us
To think
We "did it" ourselves.

Your quiet
Inward smile
Leads me
To ever greater
Reverence
For all that
You have painstakingly
Learned
And now share freely
With us.

Ocelia,
You are at once
The butterfly
In the golden sunlight
And the rock
Upon which you alight.

You are
The ever renewed
Flowers of spring
And the fresh air
That carries
The fragrance of
Your love
To me and all else
Under the sun.

Even that which
I cannot see
Benefits
From your
Benevolent care.

I am proud to be
Your tree
The loving home
Of your singing
Bird,
The guarantor
Of your annual
Nest.

And even if you
Fly away
Where my roots
Cannot follow
I know
Without a doubt
We are always
In each other's
Hearts.

# Guardian Angel

amp, cool and smooth
Is this small flattened boulder
Touching bare skin
Deep in canyon lost
Where one can be found
Only by deer track
And calling bird.

The long haired
Slick green moss waves
In the lazy current of cool waters
Far beneath the bowered oak
And castled walls
Overhung by Nature's
Own bonsai pines and firs.

Mosses happily sow green
Their furry carpets soft
While the tiniest
Of mountain springlets sings
Time honored lullabys
So delicate the crash
Of a falling leaf
Can drown out easily
A phrase but temporary.

Not a soulword is lost,
For the listening bush wren
Chimes the muffled notes gentle true
For geriatric root knarled bark
And newcomer alike.

And why not,
This small plain
Brownish feathered flier has heard
The stories a million times before
And besides, she isn't going anywhere
For the moment at least;
All her little ones
Are fast asleep
Kept safe covered
By her freckled breast.

II

Stretching slightly,
The child's wing moves
Just enough allowing
Two bright blue eyes
A view over the edge
Of that cool well worn rock
In time to spy
A small group of fingerlings
As they turn on their sides
To wave at him
With a flash of scale
Found by the smallest piece
Of sunlight given occasional
Access through leafy cloud
By breeze caprice.

III

Each being here sentient
Having been found whole
Though not entirely understood
By a racing populace outside
Not bent on knowing the mystery
That is themselves,
Are forever wedded

To this tiny island
Hidden away forgotten
Again and again
Until one more time
That which Is rises up
Out of seeming ruin
To witness itself in the void,
Where it is actually
Become quite crowded.

IV

Each particle of energy round
Is given a body of expression
A functional storied role
A place to sing with heart
All possible colors
In a nonlinear formula
That always arrives
At the One.
So much of life around me
Has the answers aware
And they await, singing patiently,
The great awakening.

V

See the grasses wave and heel
Before the wind among them
As it barges across the meadow
Surprising the delicate long stems
Of pale bright flowers
Integrated from day one.

They toss their heads smartly
Saying yes to all
Denying no one
A taste of their stories.

It is all here.
From branch to leaf
From bird to ant
And cloud to hill
All sing in unison
For the Love that pours out
Of the universe
And fills every corner of Creation.

VI
In the wild
Find I peace
And succor mild,
Wherein is ease
For inner child.

In quiet eye
Is the broadcast expanse
Of Mother at her best,
She makes no move
To hide the Truth
Though you seldom see
Her stop to rest.

Eternal music
Of the spheres
Blends me whole
Drowns errant fears,
And heals the birthplace
Of all my tears.

A daily shepherd sun
Salutes the broken effort
And warms inside shadows
Of such a one,
And proves there is no end
To what was not begun.

That sanguine surrender
Is now close by,
Its fire is cradled
In Love divine
Of sea, earth and sky.

VII
This then, is the field.

A common ground for understanding
Where we meet as equals,
To listen intently to the Word
Often expressed through someone else.

Yet new Truth revealed personal
A little something for each
To place close to our hearts,
An awkward fit at first
To be taken out
And studied in private gently
Without judgement's rush to scald.

There is constant assistance
In this work.
If I but ask allowing to receive
The happiness and joy,
Regulated only
By what smallness accepts.

VIII
An ebullient cascade
In constant shower,
And now I know it's here.

# Touch

heels of life
Reach for the road
One last chance just run away
For heart to find the dawn,
And freedom's blush of soul
Hard to rightly say
From where it might've come.

I watch an early breeze
Steal the shadow's chill
And give it to the sun,
Laughter takes its ease
While feathered gypsies
Make their plans
Gathered on the run.

All this eons chase
One generation to the next.
Covers the truth about the path
And leaves an empty nest.

Wisdom's word says journey's end
Begins within where Self is found.
Universe reaches out with love
And in the light is darkness drowned.

Stillness gone to ground in silence fair
Pause to take ahold,
Of gibbous place between our thoughts
Plant your seed in summer's warmth
Not in winter's cold.

Clouds arrive midday
To cool the sunny blast.
Desert souls breathe relief
The monsoon die is cast.

Laying down close to Mother Earth
Belly in the mud,
I take time to receive
Her message in my blood.

"Slow down my little one
Swim downstream to the sea,
I have ways of healing you
And you of healing me."

"Pay no attention to carrion beast
For it is just their job,
Feast not upon the food of death
Or become the bloody mob."

"Remain close hid alive
The angels live among,
For in the light He gives to you
Cherished friends will surely come."

"The work you agreed to do
While still in stratosphere
Was not meant for somewhere else
But to complete today, right here."

Scattered raindrops land on leaves
Others hit the ground
Songbird calls for more to come
A cloud the wind has found.

Butterflies each pump
Their allotted drop of blood,
The wings they wave in unison
Is cause for aerie flood.

I am taken to my inner self
Grow accustomed to the might
And grateful cheer most heartily
The clearing of my sight.

Huge clouds draw close
Wind goes slack
As anvils do they make,
Thor's weighty hammer lightning strikes
Done for all life's thirsty sake.

The downpour starts but gently first
Catch basin runoff filled,
Smiling faces dance in branch and leaf
Fears of drought are stilled.

Tears no longer held inside
Joined to gentle rain,
Are for laughter mixed with joy
So good to be One again.

Flagstone floors and old stone walls
Next to garden testify,
To strength of purpose lifelong true
Led by inner Eye.

A storm laden afternoon
Early evening does overtake,
I feel washed clean like the leaves
'Tis meant for all,
Not just a lucky break.

Homeward stork flies past
A cloudy break of sky,
The last of this day's sun
Shines through
I'm left with knowing why.

Rainbow bend upon the land
With a blend of liquid light,
Mother's pulse is tuned to heal
I stand in freedom's sight.

My sojourn here this time around
Is to make ready the journey home,
With endeavor built to last
This will be the one.

An enlightened moment is at the end
Of this my rocky trail,
The vision shines within me yet
For Maker never fails.

At first I didn't understand the gift
Later it felt too much,
But then the muddle of it all
Was set to right
By mystery's graceful touch.

# A Letter To William Tell

Dear Bill,

knows everyone up here
And had a place all set aside
Before we even arrived.
I'm getting civilized.
She's got me living inside
A box called an apartment
With a real bathroom and everything.
There is a cookroom
That has a vitrified bucket
With a hole in it called a drain.
The water disappears into the wall
And won't come back.
O said it's supposed to be like that
And it is okay to get more water
Any time I want.
She showed me
The little whirly gadget on the wall too
And that is where
The water comes back out.
I wanted to know why
The water wasn't all soapy –
She just threw up her hands
And said that's the way
It works here in town.
After a while,
I figured there must be a filter
In the wall somewhere.
She just looked at me

Like I was tetched in the head
And said to stop using big words.
We got a new music box.
Now I don't have to hum to myself.
It even talks out loud.
O says to go ahead
And let it speak,
'Cause when I  talk to myself,
It makes the neighbors nervous;
Especially when I know the answers
To my own questions.

There is the funniest little stove
In the cookroom.
It has four spirals on top of it
And when you turn
The little whirly things on the front,
The spirals get red.
I put the firewood on top
Like a good boy
'Cause I wanted to cook something to eat.
For such a little stove,
It made an awful lot of smoke
So I opened up
All the doors and windows
But the smoke arrester hollered anyway.
About then, some fellers showed up
In a big red hurry up wagon.
I invited them in for supper
But they didn't want to sit down
And made me go outside.
That was okay as I like it there,
But here was this great big stranger
Pacing up and down
In front of the wagon.
He seemed awfully nervous,

Especially when I asked
After his large red hat.
I was curious to know
What kind of cowboy he was
As I'd never seen anything like it.
That's when I heard
His music box talk.
He turned around,
Listened real close and then answered it.
I told him not to let people
See him do that,
They might think it would be a good idea
If he wasn't in charge.
He just turned around
And looked at me in the strangest way.
When he realized I was serious
All the wrinkles smoothed out of his forehead,
His shoulders dropped
And for a minute I thought
He was gonna cry.
Then he puffed up
And wanted to know "who the hell"
I thought I was.
I told him I was Omanasa's man,
But that she wasn't here just now.
He spun me around
And introduced me to a friend of his.
This feller was dressed all in blue
But I knew he was a cowboy right off.
He had a gun and everything.
I spoke right up
And said howdy pardner
And then I pointed my finger
At him real fast and said "draw!"
He jumped back
And put his hand on his gun

But then realized I had the drop on him.
It was a moment
Before those two eased up,
But then they somehow laughed
Without smiling.
The red cowboy said
I should go with the blue cowboy
So I told Red
To go on ahead inside
And serve up dinner before it got cold
And that we'd be back after a bit.
That red cowboy was odd.
I never seen anyone wave goodby
By shaking their head.

Anyhow, I went with the blue cowboy
Over to his shiny new car.
I remarked it must be
A real nice outfit he worked for
As they had their brand on his door.
He walked me around to the other side
And wonder of wonders,
He had him a brand on that door too.
He opened it up
And helped me inside real polite like.
He even held the top of my head
So I wouldn't bang it.
That's when I decided
I liked him as he was such a gentleman
And I spoke right up
And let him know.
He thanked me
But said just the same
I wasn't to touch anything.

He got in on his side
And right off
Started talking to his music box.

I was going to say something,
But I figured it made him happy
So what the heck.
Pretty soon,
I wanted to know where we were going
And he said to some place
Called the Funny Farm.
I asked what kind of animals
They had there
And he said all kinds.
I said oh good, will they let me feed some of them?
He just busted out laughing.
I remarked
It must be a real funny place.
He said it was a real zoo.

It was getting dark
As we arrived at a tall gate
And an even taller fence
That went around this big building
With bright lights.
There was this big tall mean looking feller
Beside the gate.
He stepped forward
And growled at the blue cowboy
And wanted to know who was the yayhoo
In the car with him.
I told that loudmouth
To watch his step
'Cause the blue cowboy was my friend
And if he was gonna hurt him
He would have to deal with me first.
Those two took to laughing so hard
Tears run down their cheeks.
I could tell they were beginning
To see things my way,
So I relaxed back into the seat.

The blue cowboy drove on up
To the front door
And took me inside.
We went over
To this long skinny tall table
That looked like
It was nailed down to the floor
Where a ranch hand
Was sitting behind it.
He was dressed all in white.
That's when I noticed
Everything was white
Except the floor.
It was all checkerboard,
Wall to wall.

The white cowboy wanted to know
Why I was here.
Blue said
I called him Blue now
'Cause we was friends
Blue said
I was there for observation,
Whatever that meant.
I asked the white cowboy
Where were the checkers
Since he was sitting down
We might as well have us a match.
He looked at me like I was nuts
But I just pointed at the floor
And put him on notice
I was a pretty fair hand
At the game myself.
I didn't allow
As to get big headed though,
I figured anybody

With a board that big
Must play a lot.

The white cowboy stood up
And pointed me at a door
So I shook Blue's hand
And thanked him very much
For bringing me
All the way out here
To such a fine farm.
He looked at the white cowboy
With a pained expression
Then turned and walked away.

The white cowboy
Made the door buzz real loud
Like a rattlesnake
But it opened anyway
And he told me to go on in.
I peered through the opening
Looking for that snake
Or any other critters for that matter,
But there weren't any.
He put me
In another white room
And said the doctor
Would see me shortly.
That's when I heard a commotion goin' on
Down the hall.
I guessed out loud
The boys must be bustin' broncs.
As the white cowboy
Dashed off
He muttered something about
Ol' Bob was at it again,
And that I was to stay

In that room no matter what
And not touch anything.
I thought that was odd
As there wasn't anything in here.
Not even any checkers.

So I sat down on the floor.
For a long time.
After a while
I started goin' over
My best checker moves,
Sort of hopscotch like.
That's when I saw the mirror.
It gave me an idea.
I went over to it
And looked behind me
At the checkered floor.
I figured there might be
Some advantage to seein'
The game backwards
Sort of like
The other guy's point of view.
Well, I was studyin'
The situation real hard
When I realized that the mirror
Was built into the wall.
I thought that strange at first
But figured they didn't want to take
A Chance on having it fall and break.
Somebody might have
Seven years bad luck.
I was lookin' at that mirror
Real up close when I thought
I saw somethin' move.
I turned around real fast
But there wasn't anybody there.

I looked back at the mirror again.
There it was.
It must have been a ghost
'Cause it made the hair stand up on the back of my neck.
Then the mirror got dark
Like someone had turned out a light.
I jumped back
And exxed myself religiously,
Just in case.
In a moment
The door to the room I was in
Opened up behind me
And that same white cowboy came in,
Carrying two chairs.
Following him was another white cowboy
With a flat piece of wood
In his hands
That had a piece of paper
Stuck on it.
Most curious.
The second white cowboy
Thanked the first white cowboy
And said he'd better go
And check up on Bob again.
As he left, the second cowboy
Pointed to a chair
And said to sit down.
So I did.
He sat in the other chair
And began to look at me
Most closely
Through his thick round glasses.
They made his eyes look real big
And swim around on his face.
After a while
I was beginning to get seasick
When he spoke.

He said he was doctor Trowbridge
And that no one
Was going to hurt me.
I said that wouldn't be necessary
As I didn't believe
In hurting animals
Even on his farm
And for him not to give it
A second thought.
He just looked at me blankly
And then wrote something
Down on his board.
He began to ask me questions.
They had to do with
How I would take it
If I lost my job.
That was easy.
I'd never had one.
He wanted to know
If I liked people.
I said yes,
Everyday.
He wanted to know
If I could read and write.
I looked him straight in the eye
And said no;
I could understand
What the animals were saying,
But it had never occurred to me
To write any of it down.
They liked my jokes though.
He went on and on.

By now he had filled up
Two pieces of paper
And looking at his watch

Said we had been talking
For three hours.
He wanted to know
If that meant anything to me.
I said one day into the next
Was all the same to me.
And that I wasn't
In any sort of hurry.
He cleared his throat
And abruptly stood up.
He went over to the door
And opened it
Gesturing for me to follow.
We went back to that snake door
And with a loud buzzing sound
It opened up all by itself.
We went out into the big white room
Past the long skinny table
And the first cowboy
Who was leaning on it
Like he was tired.
He had a wet towel up to his head
And when he removed it
I could see
He had a big black eye.
It was swollen and purple too.
I told him
Bustin' bronc's was a dangerous business
And just because
We didn't hit animals
Didn't mean they wouldn't hit us.
He just moaned
And swallowed some more
Little white things.

Just then,
The blue cowboy entered the front door.

He had O with him.
She and I ran toward each other
And hugged all over.
I could tell she was real worried.
Blue looked
At the second white cowboy
And then back at O and me.
Then back at the cowboy.
He said he'd received a call
To come pick me up
But wanted to know why.
Obviously there had been
Some kind of mistake.
Surely they could see
I was bananas
And needed some kind of help,
And that I should be staying there.
Nope, no mistake they said.
He is sound as a dollar,
Just lives in a different world
We don't understand:
And with all the budget cuts,
There just isn't any room
For him here.

With that,
I cheerfully waved goodby
To the two white cowboys
And walked toward the big front door
With O and Blue.
I took Blue by his big right hand
And looked him straight in the eye
And with a stiff upper lip
Told him not to feel bad,
It wasn't the first time
I'd been turned down for a job.

# Thankful

lowing down came easier
As he passed through life's elder door,
The coming twilight gave him
Pause to stop and reflect
Upon so much to be thankful for.

He remembered when illusion's fist
First hit him in the face,
He then saw so much more.
And dropping slowly from the race,
Turned, and went through a different sort of door.

The Light revealed our own true Love
Which came to us from within.
And right away he saw at last
His only goal was in the heart
Where we always forever win.

Safe at last the strength to carry on
Came on rushing in.
And experience showed divine protection
Never was commodity.
For there, darkness found profit margin thin.

Taking heart he studied hard
Put in long hours both day and night,
He saw the best way
To win Freedom's war
Was without starting up a fight.

He saw the bloody battleground within the human mind
For it was plugged with dark debris,
He took the sword of Truth and cut the cord
There anyway that blind lead maggot blind
And spread the Light upon our Souls, there, for all to see.

Saying, here's for you and you and you
I don't do this just for me,
Come on, climb out your tunnel dark
Leave misery's muck and join the living in the Light
And learn to Love and Be.

With the Truth as life's most treasured Light
Turn over ignorance cart,
And free those children trapped in there
It has no right to bind,
Come on in to God, be your Spirit's part.

When he came upon the lust of flesh
Truth made its waxy skin to rot,
Then before us he kissed the children there
Who had fallen in that darkest trap
And the Light of Love wrote chapter two, of the golden plot.

Taking stock once again of all that
Which he saw to be grateful for,
He sang out loud as a tiny spark lit up inside
New Love for our inner child
Continued to tally up the score.

The road was straight the day was clear
When the dragon rose up and put children on the run,
He stood fast in Freedom's wake
And sent fear forever back to its home in oblivion.

And there on the edge of unknown loss
He caused anger to leave its storm,
And taught all who would listen there

To eat the apple
But not the worm.

From there he tempered his sword of Truth
With forgiveness, counseled those who came to call,
And wherever he went spread the Word of Love
Because the more we make the more there is,
The cornucopia spreads for all.

The deadly sins were running now
Hiding from his sight,
But the shadows gave them up
For they too were just another form,
Of that perpetual guiding Light.

Then that final beast rose up
In its blinded ignorant rage,
It grabbed him both cold and hot
But was unable, to put him, in a cage.

The people spoke hushed at first
Then their Spirits awoke as One,
Saying he is us and we are he
Your disaster kills tomorrow's child
Your lie, has come undone.

But the beast refused to listen
He'd been built without reverse,
And to all
He made pollution glisten
He said, this will be your curse.

Then the sainted one upon the beast
Blew his darkest darkest Love,
And the dead machine
Who thought he knew it all,
Became, the whitest dove.

# Lefty The Tulip

hat a beautiful
Flower you are.
Standing here
In this world
With a fragrance
So delicate
Only a slow moving
Quiet nose
Would notice;
Your nectar
Long robbed
By busy workers,
And pollen
Scattered
To the four winds.
The tips of your
Petals
Are beginning to curl
With age
And a drooping
Stem
Strains to hold
Your blush
Aloft
While the silent riot
Of your singular face
Easily compares
To the clearest
Of any
Sunrise.

With leaves
And stem
Of gentlest
Greens
Becoming
The seashell
Pinks
Of the very
Grandest of
Dreams,
One realizes
There is no
End to you
No dungheap
Of forgetfulness
Possible.
Your perfection
Raises me
For all time
And again I am
Reminded,
No one,
Is ever
Alone.

# First Haiku, Now This

SPRING

elt snow fills the creek
Its noisy laugh floods the sky
And wears away stones

Staring at the ground
Small pebbles in my shadow
Call to take them home

The clear drop of dew
Hidden beneath leafy hair
Shows all, the blue sky

Sprite breeze curls the leaves
The last patch of shady snow
Gives spring a final chill.

Meanwhile back in town
Sidewalk cracks filled to bursting
The ants steal your sugar

SUMMER

The lazy fly fell
Off the table's edge too late
To save itself again

Hot sun sets orange
Our cat woke up to the night
Even the street slowed down

Garden is heavy
Small town life is ever so sweet
And so is the air

Mist with no promise
Veils the sun poorly and gets
Snagged by our mountain

The year burns its fuse,
With the midpoint come and gone
Days become shorter


AUTUMN

Horizon on fire
Our cat licks a purple spill
Who says its over?

Rosy cheek children
Jumping in piles of brown leaves
Grey mouse, wants to sleep

Holiday's hover
And the mouths eye the pies
Homework forgotten

A frosty wind blows
Leaving many trees naked
The full moon pulls me

Young kidjet dives deep
Into the stream, bugs beware
He walks the bottom

WINTER

In order to eat
Raven drops walnuts on the curb
Raw honey for sale

First snow starts to fall,
With the last of the food gone
She-bear goes to sleep

Memory's picture
Of yesteryear can't block out
Wheels of falling snow

Red and blue snowbirds
Watch me for seeds as my boot
Crunches the silence

Lovers give gladly
To laughter's romance as it
Makes snowbound go easy

# Ithuriel's Spear

he rain of daylight
Differs from rain after dark
My heart knows the Truth.

By nature I am
Living in the way of Love
All Life long is Now.

Listening inside
Makes everything come easy:
A clap of thunder!

Quiet solitude
Sounds like being all alone,
But I never am.

The One and only
Which we are always imparting
Fills voids of myself.

Your song and my song
May not ever sound the same,
Crane flies with both wings.

The river which is
Life with no expectations
Flows without struggle.

Swans paddle fish swim
Reeds bend people grow with love
What a big lovely.

Stars shine upon me,
The silence is my best friend
So do all of you.

Wind blows the snowdrifts
From ragged mountain ridges,
Bare feet smooth stone floors.

Night sky with no moon;
Flower's light is my lantern,
Horse knows the way home.

Dry needles of pine
Are each yesterday's moments,
Tomorrow's next breath.

Love settles around,
But could never be accused
Of being mere dust.

Cub's roly poly
Rough and tumble down the slope,
Land in mother's nap!

My neighbor's laughter
Filters through these silent walls
Their mirth is my bones.

The beginner's flute
Like the exuberant child
Makes fresh the Way Home.

My new found friend Joy
Sleeps beside me on the bed:
A kitty of course.

I look to the sky
But inside is where I go
To spark Love and Peace.

Loss is not real,
Especially when nothing
Belongs to me here.

My life is charged
With anticipation now
But not with outcome.

When I remember
To love, I learn what it is
To be authentic.

The last time I went
To the store it was still there,
But the grapes were gone.

# Homage To A Runaway Train

an you hear the clouds
The clouds they are a cryin',
But not for sadness
Do they roam.
Their tears are shed
In gladness,
For Joy they weep this very day,
We are going home.

Is your heart among the mountains
Singing laughter's song,
My heart is bursting open
Love can do no wrong.
Our sun shines upon tear stained cheeks,
My tears fill the little creeks
Who join together down the hill
And make the rivers strong.

The Devas dance around us
I see them with the Fauns,
They are singing for The Great One
God Is the coming dawn.
Pine Tree and Strawberry
Race each other laughing to the prize,
I am humbled by their meaning
We are joining with the wise.

Quan Yin, she favors me
I cannot tell you why,
I am slow awakening

There's something in my eye.
With ringings loud within my ears
The moment slows a wayward child,
I stand transfixed in the Light,
Of her ageless golden smile.

Those three days
Will always special special be,
You asked would I please come,
And there in Joy I found my family,
With the Mighty One.
It is the closest I've ever been
To others deep in Love,
The Ascended Masters too were there
And gave my heart a shove.

I miss you all so very much
It feels like flesh without its skin,
I know our universe is rather small,
And before too long, I'll be with all of you again.
It snowed it rained and was gray
Just for us the sun did shine,
I thank you for your Loving hearts
Given unto me, so I could make them mine.

# That Little Round Mound

It is a particular place
I often picture in my mind,
There are many beings there
Some were long to find.
And some are small and quiet like
And to a fault are very kind
While other's patience knows no bounds
To them I go for comfort's sake
For there my soul unwinds.

Brother Pine so very near who guards
That which we learn to give away
Has a laughter all his own
He freely shares, both by night, and day.
I love to bask within his Light.
Where my child can safely play,
And it is to this open door I go in peace
And enter there within,
Where I'm always begged to stay.

My home has ever surrounded me
The entrance is in my heart;
Long knowing has served me well
Reminding where to start.
Another child asked me once
Please show us this special part,
I found the words in front of me
And said go unto that little hill,
And open up your heart.

# Touched By Starlight

aters ice pure
Sunrise pinkish glow
Are gifts left unto me
From dreams
The night before.

Where touched by spirit
Through my heart
The sprinkled heavens
Were found deep inside
A friendly afterglow.

The tiny mountain spring
Was born to sing
Even when covered with ice
And buried deep
In winter's whitest snow.

I listened close
To Mother's muse
With friends who
Never went to town –
There is no need to go.

Close hid among the souls
Who lay wide open
In the flower of newborn old
Are the cherished ones
Who've learned to live in love
And also how to grow.

With the polished sparkle
Of newest dew in his eye
Eagle soars the highest heights
And leaves the mountain tops
Far away below.

And all this while
The tiny silver voice
Who sings of starlight pure
Is God's Whole Truth
In the hungry face
Of human rush and flow.

# Dream Wheel

idden falls
Among the pines
Is where I often go
(to be) With trackless minds.
The rainbows in
Their rising mists
Remind me go
Among rooted twists
And loose my tears
Upon the moss;
But weep I not,
For material loss.
I know instead
That I am loved
By the Mighty One
Up above
And also here and there
God can be found
In everything and everywhere.

My tears are shed –
I found mySelf
And am always met
By the nearest Elf
Who glows bright
In the silent void
Of the One Great Heart
Never devoid
Of Love for all
Be it man or beast

Quiet plant
Or image least.
Here behind
The falling water
I give all my woes
It doesn't matter
To the thunder's damp
And springtime's wonder
So darkness' spell
I'm out from under
Into the yield
Of sunlit Truth
I walk the field
The field of youth.

# Going, Going, Gone

s my footprints slow let go
Their mark upon the forest floor
And afternoon softens
The mighty glare
I'm given over to the quiet shadows
And gentle breeze who scatters
The tattered and lifeless leaves
In this ancient place,
Old, long before the birth of flowers.
In my life's few fleeting hours
I do my best to love the failures
Which are really little triumphs,
In and all their own.
The evening's chill rolls down
From upper Loveland hill
And gives my heel a little nip
To remind the rest
Of the tiny glow from cabin's lamp
And the soft sweet voice
Of my Love,
As she skips across
A perfect singing floor.
Old bear of black sniffing for my track
Is up ahead near Silver Spring,
He knows for him I have honey.
The bees in their buzzing lair
All knew I'm without a care
And to my branch some sweetness stuck
Needing nothing in return,
But ask for love and never money.

Our bear who knows I'm here
Sits down to relax
Beside our favorite rock,
And waits patient for the gift.
He hugs me gently back
And for a while we sit and talk
About matters to the 'fore;
And it's his opinion I garner close
For he is the forest's designated host
Grandfather's brother, keeper and lifelong friend.
With spritely cuff from sticky paw
I bid farewell and slow withdraw
To continue on to my new home
The place a forest glade
Below Silver Spring
Where blood picks up its fervent pace
To the beat of ancient drums.

It is there God wed His Mistress fair,
I find it peaceful
All around and run
Into the arms of my Love
Whose waiting country my eyes implore
And a lingering kiss my lips endure
Upon her cheek my tears
Are made to fall
She knows this life for me was hard
But that's all over now
My Angel takes me Home.

# The Only Treasure

ike a breath of fresh air
After an unusually hot
Sticky day
My heart blooms anew
In sanguine unhurried love

Roller coasters of the unknown
No longer pull at my eyes
Nor do
Heat waves of ambition
Inhibit the dove

Lost to the mountain's sweet song
Long gone are the snowy white cloud's
Rainy perfume
I swoon to the angel's caress
From high up above

The new found freedom to grow
Along with not being afraid
Proffers the gift
So recent discovered to serve
Goes hand in the glove

Wave upon wave of identical bird
School in the current of life
Make it just so;
All hearts open as one
The only treasure is love

# Brave Warrior
# Of The Western Meadow

orning's first leaf
Opened a tentative pore
Then felt about
And opened some more

The damp in the ground
Rose up in the air
Becoming a mist
Scented so fair

Critters used to the dark
Left in silence the night
Their majesty lures
The coming of light

First rays of dawn
Give substance to thought
Those who scamper away
Do not wish to be caught

The works that we do
Lives that we live
Are all subject to Love
And the service we give

I'm learning to love
Myself more every day
Consensus is now
To keep it that way

Healing of all else
Rests in beginning at home
Each changes the world
By sprouting alone

The first ray of dawn
Lays warmth on my cheek
Spills all over the flowers
Down by the creek

Creek leads the breeze
On to the lake
Where mountain reflects
Just for our sake

Canadian geese
Look to the North
They know what the moon
Is about to bring forth

With the ease of a pro
They mount currents on high
And calling encouragement
Add grace to the sky

I'm left behind
Not forgotten you know
My heart flies with them
Wherever they go

Now I'm content
To be with the trees
Their intimate air
Puts me at ease

It feels so good
To finely slow down
I may never go back
To the hurry of town

With sincere intent
To open my heart
I'm safe here at last
No more apart

Nature opens her gate
In reverence pass in
It's good to be home
In silence again

By just letting go
Of my will to control
I'm given the Light
Of the Fourth World

My higher Self
Who's been all along
Congratulates me
Brave and so strong

I'm looking forward
To being with God
Silly ol' me
I've been on the nod

Now once again
A life with no pain
I'm careful to take
Very good aim

I've been here before
My heart it can see
The wonder White Light
Coming closer to me

Now is the time
Go ahead surrender the last
That barrier down
I'm free now to pass

All of the Masters
Go through this same door
Don't worry they're back
To help us some more

Don't fret your mind
If it gets blown
It's only the Truth
You're being shown

Separate's not real
There is nothing to fear
You are so Loved
God is right here

# Vinegar Man

Standing here holding the ancient tools
    of primal birth,
And gazing at our very own ageless
    Mountain Maiden
So tall behind God's wayward trees
    Whose leaves perpetually wave farewell
  to the artful wind,
A hot tear falls in gratitude but
Is not lost to the healing mothers.
Our lady of the faultless sky,
Her steep slopes still covered by last winter's white,
Ruby bedazzled by the cast of our best setting sun
Lives the true monarchy
Unobtainable except with our hearts,
Holds within hers,
The bonding of our Love and bestows upon me
All the family I could ever want.
Never lost am I among the countless folds
Of her unanimous tresses, where I go to lose
All thought and sound of vagary
Brought on by my outside mental din.
This is not an away from, but a moving to
A headlong heartfelt rush into clarity,
Where one's sanity is no longer the Jokers's commodity
Or charismatic possession of any bracketed lifestyle.
Many's the time have I brought a broken, exhausted,
Grief stained tragedy to my Mother's knee,
There to be comforted; and in time am I sent forward
Laughing joyfully with a perfectly mended heart.
Not in so many words does she speak to me.

Rather, it is more a pure sweet singing voice,
Accompanied
By the baritones of the lichen covered boulders
And testaments
Proclaimed in counterpoint by virile trees
And all the animal inhabitants who are cloistered
In this edgeless boundary free entanglement.
The other spirits who adorn her, eye me with
Their gentle concern and non judging discrimination,
Patiently awaiting the day when my awareness
Joins theirs equally.
I too, look forward to this place where upon awakening,
My mystic constructs will have come into their own.
"If not the originator, then a joiner be,"
Say the snowflakes.
It quickens me peacefully to hear so many voices
In the silence,
Where I went for what seemed just a few moments
But turned out to be a seeming eternity.
Happy was I to find myself once again in waiting
To my regal Lady.
Long absent had the diversions become.
Dropped out of the imaginary race for lack of players.
I guess.

And still, her music carries on,
In the hollows and quiet valleys of my soul.
It feels wonderful to be back, although I hadn't really gone.
More like self discipline having found its throne,
Along with the attendant birth
Of a singularly unique phenomenon
Known as self esteem
And the loving calmness of awaking to the remembrance,
Of who I really am, and why I came.

# Feral Child

ittle one
Warm asleep
Surrounded by dogs
Both great and small
Who work
His family's world
Found somewhere
Near timberline
On the Roan plateau,
Stirs in his bed
Made from
Two woolies' hides
Roughly laced
Together
With rawhide
Set off with
Hammered conchos
Made of Spanish
Silver.

The young child
With sleepy eyes
Reaches over
And lays
A small hand
Affectionately
Upon the left
Foreleg
Of old Bull
The giant sheepdog

Who crouches
Next to him
Facing East
Awaiting
The rising
Sun.
The wet black
Twitching nose
Is all you can see
Of the great dog's
Greying muzzle
As it samples
The chill air –
Crisp and dry
High desert pure.
Bull,
Still as a stone
Lowers his head
Licks the hand
And then the arm
And quickly pins
The man pup
With one huge paw
Preventing him
From wiggling
Down into
His sheepskin
Bag to hide
And thoroughly
Washes the small
Blue eyed face
With a most
Gentle patient tongue.
With that done,
I crawl out
Of my bed

And stand naked
Next to my
Friend and protector
Rubbing my face
Dry
In the fur
Of his neck.

Still crouching,
Bull is taller
Than I.
He has gone back
To witness
Our rising sun.
With my arm around
His warm neck
I gaze up to watch
Our nighttime friends
Blink out
One by one
As my roof, the sky,
Begins slowly
At first to pink
The Eastern clouds.
There is seldom
Any true silence
Here on the plateau.
The wildlife teeming
In the meadows
And sagebrush forest
That covers
The slopes
And rocky places
Are an ancient
Society
Long used

To conversation.
Even the early
Butterfly
Has a unique
Song to sing
As she slowly
Opens and closes
Her wings
Drying them
And pumping her tiny
Allotment of blood.
Chado.
My Indian brother,
Has taught me
How to listen
And proved to me that
I can never
Be alone.
The sound of
Bossey's bell
As she shakes
Her head
Brings me back
To my self
And I quickly
Slip into my
Pants and moccasins.
Over at the campfire
Next to our wagon
Gramm gives me
A hot bowl
Of oatmeal
With a dollop
Of brown sugar
On it and I dash off
To Bossey

For the best part.
She's a blue cow,
Revered by
Everyone around
For she knows
The weather
And all its moods.
In times
Of uncertain change
All the animals
Follow her
To safe haven,
Even the antelope
And deer.
She is standing
In the middle
Of the herd
And I slow
To a walk
Skirting the sheep
Mostly ewes
With lambs
Still bedded down
In the dark meadow.
I can hear
The splish splish
Of her milk
In the pail
As Gramps works
Her pliant udder
With his
Stong fingers.
She knows it's me
And lows softly
As I gently
Lean my head

Against her belly.
She is warm
And smells
Like the meadow.
Her milk is rich
And almost hot.
Gramps is filling
My bowl also
And hands it
Back full
Without missing
A beat.
Bossey gives more
Than a large pail
Of milk
Twice a day,
Plenty
For all of us,
Including Blackie,
Her calf
Who is almost
Weaned now
And would rather
Eat flowers
And sweet
Meadow grass
Anyway.
It is early summer
And everything
Is in full bloom.
The lambs
Are growing fast.
During the daytime
They wander
Further from
Their mothers now

And cavort together
In the meadows
Delighting
In surprising
Flocks of small
Light blue
Butterflies,
Always under the
Ever watchful eyes
Of Bull, Bear and Sis.
Chado brings Waco
Our mule
Into camp
And begins
Harnessing him
To the wagon.
Waco stamps
One huge foot
And snorts at me
While lowering his nose
Into the feedbag
Full of oats
As I help slip
The loop over behind
His long ears.
Waco is spirited
But doesn't spook
Easily.
His large grey-green
Eyes always soft
Towards me
Give thanks.
Chado has
Finished with
The harness
And steps around

The wagon
To the fire
And a hot bowl
Of oatmeal
Eggs and sausage.
Bear and Sis
Have also come in
With him and now
Launch into
Their portions
Of the hot stew
That is always
Ready for them.
Gramps comes in
With the full milk pail
And grabbing
Some sausages
For his pocket
Goes out on point
After Bull, who has
Already eaten.
I help Gramm
Break camp
While the terriers
Attack their stew
With boisterous
Gusto.
They are a
Wild Bunch,
Animated and fiercely
Loyal,
A wirehaired terrier
Is small for a dog,
Swarthy
And long on stamina.
Their tenacity

Is balanced with
A cunning
Intelligence,
And when
A pack of them
Are after
A predator
They are more like
A bunch of
Fur covered Piranhas.
With me, they are
Frisky, noisy
And playful,
But become
All business
And bandy legged
When gramp walks past
Pointing at me
And says, "Watch'em."
Gramm climbs up
Onto the wagon seat
And with
A gentle rein
Bids Waco
To pull away.
I was given a choice
To ride or stay
With Chado
And the herd,
Knowing I usually
Choose the latter.
As the wagon moves out,
I'm reminded
To collect
Wild spinach
And Lamb's Quarters

For supper.
Chado finishes
His cup of strong
Black coffee
And walks back
Into the milling
Herd
Looking for anything
That may not
Be right.
Satisfied, he speaks
Softly with Gramp
In his gentle
Ageless voice
Agreeing to move
The animals
North to Cold Spring
Where we will
Meet up with Gramm
And fresh water.
The sun breaks free
Of the horizon
Just as Gramp
Signals Bull
Bear and Sis
To push
The herd on.
With much commotion,
The ewes call
Their young to them
Before moving
Off from where
They bedded down
The night before.
With everyone found
And accounted for,

The fat fleecy
Mass bursts forward
The fifty yards
To untrampled meadow
There to begin
Eating their way
The three miles
To Cold Spring.
It is a good year
For feed and
The weather is fair.
The snows
Of last winter
Still cling
To the rocky peaks.
Their meltwaters
Fill the brooks
And small streams
That criss-cross
The Roan
In lazy patterns
Temporarily left
Muddy
By the hundreds
Of small cloven
Feet that cross
The icy wetness
In search of
The tender shoots
That every year
Shout
Their promise eager.

# Child Of The Morning Mist

"Giving is receiving,"
Sparked the meadowlark,
After his singularly unique long
Rendition of everyone else's
song.
He is in the fourth year
Of this, his present life
"A maturing of appreciation."
That's what he calls it,
A most precious treasure;
being
In a mind to give,
On and on
With no end to the flow
Of life itself in sight.
He is enthusiastic
About his discovery
Knowing all the while
It isn't only his
Nor is he the author of it
That doesn't matter.
The fact remains
He is here to be the voice
This morning's local rep
Cheerfully signifying
The greater Presence,
Who Is and quickens the spirit
Found in the crisp
Early morning air,
The sparkle in the briskly

Dancing sunlight,
The smell of the wet
Sandy beach bordering
A mist covered lake,
And my own blood
Making its rounds
Through artery and vein.
Each breath topples me
With their regularity
And stable rhythm.
This alone, is enough.
But the explosion
Of gratitude
Carries me on
Into the succeeding
      moments
And I find myself
Over and over
Broadcasting my simple sentiments
Building and building
Bridge upon bridge
Like the young spiders
That fill summer skies
Miniature contrails
Tying us all together
Creating a permanent
Loss of distance.

II
Friend Meadowlark,
      warmed
To a well earned
      confidence
Displays an ease
That can be berthed
Only in ongoing
      humility,

Goes beyond dare
In revealing the
            Truth,
Freely sharing
His tiny soul
That is actually bigger
Than all outdoors.
I am regaled
And borne anew
Homed forever
In this one true
Mutual foundation
That underlays everything
            infinite
And otherwise.
Sometimes,
When I remember, like now,
A quiet moment slips in
Between the thoughts
And creates
A beatiful music
With the silence
In the surrounding void
Which in fact
Is never empty
Of the Singular Presence
That fills me
Head to toe
With a communion
Unobtainable
In any other way.
In that perfect
            moment
I am drowned
In an intimate success
Experienced unique

Upon this earth.
This heartfelt knowing
Is the same
For each of us.
Standing here
Upon the threshold
Of this the greatest
Of all gates
Admiring the myriad
Souls who first crawl
Then stand,
Arising to the
       moment
Of their boundless joy
       smiling
In their exploding hearts
Some of them
For the first time –
I am justified,
Filled content
For the first time
With satisfaction.
I, we, have done well.
And given the
       eternity
Attendant to such
An accomplishment
A silent appreciation
For patience
Wells up inside
Of me and adds
Another carefully
Uncarved block
Upon the original
Foundation of Love.
Such is this,

And many mansions more.
Aged and ageless
Is this endeavor
It is and is not
Shall be
Was and is
Forever more
The ultimate essence
Of supreme process
Now revealed
In the living cells
Of our bodies.

III
Early morning shadows
Shrink,
Content to hie themselves
Behind a faded glory
Adopting also
The beautiful silence
Which accepts
The coming day
Surrendering itself
And thereby commingling
With the unitary strength
Of our young sun
And lone, feathered troubador.
Yea,
I am completed now
Yet continue to unfold
Sharing each
And every musical note
That I am
With all of the musicans
With all of the concerts
My heart beats wild

Smashing the falsehood
Of this final screwup
Which a whole mind
Turns into an emancipation
Crowded now
With others so old
Made new again
In the light,
Of our new day.

# A Cup, Full Of Aces

The angel's light
It touches me
I'm covered full of grace,
Just in time to save
The lost of me,
Gone without a trace.

Being spared from one's
Own worst enemy
An ultimate act of saving face,
Can no longer hide
A beastie's horns
Beneath the flowered lace.

A telescopic look inside
Reveals a far flung fight,
The outer skins of inner space
Cause skeletons of yesteryear
To closet exit's mold unfold
And make my heart to race.

A bacchanal of rusted sight
Leads more than one
A merry chase,
Look out now
Your shirt's undone
Elbow broke your mother's vase.

The crash and burn
Of another learn

A  catbox like erase
Is what you pay
In cuckold fun
While keeping up the pace.

It does no good
To bolster muck
Or give a lie a brace,
That's like oregano's
Cookpot full of dung
Smelling up the place.

A look to truth's
Uncovered head
Is not too far off base,
The opposite is like
Sitting still
While pummeled with a mace.

So what I think I'll do
Is befuddle you
By getting off the case,
And stop the fool around
On solid ground
And give love, full embrace.

# La  Casa Pampas

ur red fire sunset
Pushed westward now
By the stars this night
Blows across fluted fingerholes
Hidden from my sight.
But no matter seeing with my eyes,
Your ancient music
Waves across the temple
Of my heart,
And fills aslumber skies.
So full am I
Of love lost found
No emptiness endures,
A sweet perfection
Carries everywhere
The wiliest of cures.
There is no place left,
Except inside deep
Deeper, deep
Ever closer with myself
No hurry on my passport
Adventures wild extremely felt,
Where was naught
Or so I thought, before.

II
Fire red sunset
Purples on,
Your orange blaze, all undone.
The starlit skies are home to roost

Your night now thinks
It's won.
For me there is no battle
When balance
Is finally One,
And there is safety
In the strength of softness,
Waiting for the sun.
For me, the wait is over
There is no place left to run
I'm not even looking,
For a starting gun.

III
The softened earth
Long caressed by eon's leaves
Still warm from heat of day,
Is bed enough
To soothe my dreams
And wash the wear away.
This tiny hut
Without a door
Protects the rain
From loss of bowered pore,
And saves me the view
Should I want, the shore.
A fragrant mist
Blends with the sound of life
Night returns summer's breath
With grace I am restored,
And all savanna's children
Glow with a spectral light
That  cannot be ignored.

# Sunny Day In Blesshaven

A sunny day in Blesshaven
And she gives me a hug.
I'm on my way to closer home
As cat shreds the rug.
The gypsy street is calling
Enticing a recent shrug
Along the quay, painters tip to waves
While my love gives heart a tug.

A sunny day in Blesshaven
The snow has run away
Clouds may dark tomorrow's bright
But not our run today.
Spring has long been doubling back
Winter's grasp seems here to stay
But summer knows no flower lack
And goes on planting, anyway.

A sunny day in Blesshaven
Knows fall will come to warn
That winter approaches icily
Spring's bud is facing harm.
But the flower's impatient swelling lust
Insist the sun do warm
And all the creatures underground
Arch their gilded swarm.

# In Transit

ot of the darkness
Am I, nor the grey dawn.
Though I dwell in these places
But temporary,
This is not my home.
I am in this world
Not of it.
This body isn't real
For I and all individual
Pieces of the One Child
Are more than this.
This world is my construct,
Birthed not in asking
Too much,
Rather, in asking
For far too little.
The time of no time
Is dawning.
Soon, there will be
No past –
Only now,
Which exists
Beyond time, always has
And always will.
This present moment
Is here before me
All around all
In a form
No linear construct
Could ever conceive.

This now, this home showing way
Where God continually
Calls to His Child
And waits
For all the little pieces
To answer as One,
Is the fresh breath
For a tired heart
Who blooms anew
With more than hope and faith
Amid the ruin of a world
That really isn't here
Except in the mind
Of a momentary bad dream
Of separation
Where I forgot to laugh.

I am the child of the Great Turning.
The old paper thin continuum
Crumbles before the stare
Of clarity and forgiveness.
It catches fire and dissolves
Into less than the dust
Of forgetfulness,
And is no more.
Fear no longer has
A hold on me
For life is what I am
And cannot be lost
In the face of even
The most violent illusion,
For there is no death
Or is any destruction
Possible.
It is true.
I could wander away

From the threshold
Of heaven
Only to return again
To the optimal offer
Of ultimate singularity,
But why should I?
Haven't I already had enough
Of what I am not,
And does not exist?
My calmer view
Is to turn around
Once again
And reach out
A loving hand
To all the little pieces
Like me
Who remain,
Regarding themselves
As separate still,
Shackled to a misery
And suffering
That is of our own making.
I now awaken
From my bad dream
And walk away
From all the self imposed limits
Who marshal cloudy behavior.

Give me instead
All the love
I failed to recognize,
Without the ladle of lack
And its incessant penchant
For portion control.
Perfect love received
Is my sacred right

As a Perfect Child
Of a Perfect God.
I am without sin
And now I live
Without shame or guilt
In a Godly place,
Because
I never left.
Illusion tears at me frantic
Begging gratuitously
To give it its due
But my heart is
No longer in it,
Gone now, to the light inside
Which is and reflects
All the light
Of our only Source.
Lay ye down, skeptic
For your lies to self
No longer serve.
They never did.
Only to you, poor ego,
Were your ill gotten gains aimed.

I cannot find any benefit
To your veil.
I remember now.
Unto God, I simply say
I don't know,
Please help me.
And there He is
Without fail.
I don't know how it works
And I don't care.
That would be like trying
To justify the waterfall

To the melting glacier above
While forgetting love
Just Is.
I am ready now.
Ready to quit this flaccid clime.
This situation was never meant
To be fixed
In the first place.
I feel my body fading
Along with all the gotta do's
And better hurry's.
Suddenly, restfullness divine, fills
The woulda could spaces
And the emptiness of
Material achievement
Is drowned, in the new found silence
Of nothing left to prove.
I choose instead
To bathe to my heart's content
In the voluptuous peace
That is my heritage.

# Our Story

ore than anything
Fame or fortune
Could devise, even
The epic deeds
Of gargantuan journeys
Who yet march upon
One another
Over the comely hills
Of our best bred Thoughts,
These words
These swords are desired
To convey the reality
That we haven't actually gone
Anywhere.
All is for naught,
This posturing of poses.
The blabbermouth of edification
Has only served to fill the raucous balloon
Of confused diversity
With a not so hot air
And no real substance.
Now it is time
To burst our bubble.
No more is it useful
To kid ourselves.
The value of illusion
Has been spent
And  is now rendered worthless
As a currency of moment
Forever more, period.

Instead, let us embrace
Our Father
And drop the ball
Of controversy.
No more pushing God away
With our flimsy crutch
Called time.
Our Father isn't mad at us
Nor is he impatient.
He knows that sooner or later,
We will come around
To his way of thinking
Seein' as how we are all
Of the same Mind, anyway.
It will not serve us
To be timid.

Let us just dump the past
And get on with loving.
Loving everyone
And forgiving the rest.
There.
That's it.
All together now,
Give everything away.
Give our fear to God
He will convert it to love.
Give our light away,
That is how it comes back
Bigger an brighter.
Give the things of this world freely,
We will lose nothing
As it isn't  real.
None of it.
This is how loss is avoided.
Loss simply isn't possible.

Many beings for some time now
Have been less than enthusiastic
About death come 'round
One more time.
It doesn't have to happen this way
Anymore.
Let yourself be found
By
Father,
Listen to His Will
And be satisfied with the promise kept
That outstrips
Even your wildest dreams,
Effortlessly.
Figuring it all out is not our bag
So why bother.
Pass the faith around
Let each one have their fill
There is way more than enough.
It makes a fine road to walk upon
And once embraced
Will never wear out.
It makes a dandy lantern too.
Faith will light your way
Through any stormy night
If you just let it.
Faith is the shield
Of surrender.

One square inch of it
Will protect a legion
Of souls goin' home.
Somewhere along the line
We discover the downside
Causer of our misery
Has melted away

---

We didn't see it go
And don't miss it now.
The interim freedom
Feels so good
There just isn't any room
For loss.
Terror doesn't have a chance
Anymore because
Fear can't stand up to the light;
And anyway, we aren't buying.

# Great Day In The Morning

n optimal guess
With eyes pressed
To the long glass
Of the future,
While sensibility
Remains in the
Moment
Is the dowage
Of excitement
That fills the sails
Of my curiosity
And pulls tight
The hawser
That confines
To the dock
Of  transparency,
My wanderlust
Of passion.
With anchor chain
Arusted
And ties abinded
Long chafed
And worn past thin
Now shall I slip away
With the tide
Of freedom
And dance
In the waves
Of gifted receiving
Forever enchanted

In the story
Without end.
With the sailor's pipe
I'll turn to a jig
With the rest of me,
And our love for Him
Who made us all
Will calm the storm
Before our bow
And all the stars
So shined by day
Outsparkle the sun
Never to
Fade away.
The breeze tickles
The goosebumps
Of indiscretion
Making sameness
A mockery of convention
While I only
Wish to be
A better way
Of listening
To the One Will
While living to the fullest
The unexpected.
Here I am free at last,
My chains and stays
Were only made of smoke,
And now I am
Overtaken by a Life
Unburdened with
Commodity
Or entrapment
Of any kind.
What a relief.

# It's A Given

As the lady of bugs
Wanders the petals
Of my new found
Sunlit world
Waving "good morning"
To friend flutterby,
I can feel small smiles
Of infinite light
Touch me,
Healing as they go.
I want to immediately
Share this almighty fun
With every frown and tear
I come across
And blast the cloudy day
Of forlorn slumber.
Saying this,
This is your light.
Not from afar but within.
Inside every person
Tree rock and flower
Every animal, pond
Lake and sea
Full of life,
Comes this light.
We are the mirrors
And we have been found.
Not that we were ever lost–
Only to ourselves
And each other.

The prophecies are right,
Spoken two mil ago
And now it is our turn
To be that light
Unto this world we made
And show the way back on
To ourselves
By way of our Father's gift.
Be it known that you are
The gift unto yourself
Just as I am the gift to me
As we are the gifts
To each other.
And the music of our souls
Plays on
Seemingly louder now, sweetly,
But that is because
We are finally listening to it
While the imagined din
Fades away
Along with yesteryear's
Sorrow and regret
Which also are imaginary.
Without looking back,
Let us now
Step into the One Light
For we have already been blessed
With remembrance
Of that which we never lost,
Namely our true birthright
As the Perfect Child of God,
By our Perfect Father,
Who waits for us to resume
The Truth.
For the Truth is all there is.

It is the Light
And the Love
Of the Great Way
That only gives,
Ever creating itself
And handing itSelf over freely
To everyone, whether I am
Paying attention or not.
What a gift to emulate
Our Father
And be free of contrivance
And guile,
Everlasting in
No defense necessary
On any ground.
All I ask is to be
Permanently safe
From ever going to sleep again
And forgetting to laugh.

# Nothing Left Remains

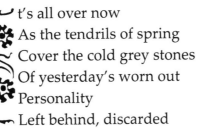t's all over now
As the tendrils of spring
Cover the cold grey stones
Of yesterday's worn out
Personality
Left behind, discarded
Of no use
To the wakened child
Laughing with his Maker
In the sunlight
While the past rapidly
Becomes unknown
Fading silently
So as not to disturb
The songs of the
Gently falling snowflakes
Who merrily proclaim
The perpetual moment
Each giving their unique
Print one above the other
To eternity
And the Love
Of which each is made.
Past civilizations
Applaud tumultuously
The awakening again
To the light
A populace peoples
Like snowmelt,
Overwhelming

The small stream
Delighted at the attention,
Forgiving the mud
Stirred up excitement
Seeing it instead as bless'ed
Opportunity.
The celestial firmament rocks
To the tune of change
As it too is remembered
For itSelf
And its effect of cause.
No longer are there
Any questions
Or need for answers
For there isn't anything
To be figured out.
Because we fooled the bad dream
And its little world
Of illusion's artifice,
Our folly's
Indiscretionary oops,
We are free
To return at any time
To our One Mind
Where we never left.
And of all this insanity,
Nothing left remains.

# In This Life

lying through the tangle
Of illusory affairs,
Yesterday is left behind.
I am each succeeding note
Of a music unheard
So new in its ageless tapestry
Woven by the One Hand.
Created fresh and stirring,
I compel you to look inside
All the way to now,
The present moment,
Which is always
Your true home
That place which is
The center of our universe
No matter where you are –
That place, you never left.

II
A golden thread
Lays across my open hand.
Grasping it not
Prevents the present
From slipping away.
The ownership of control
Can bind it not
This link to all
Which is mine
And yours and ours.
In a woven song

Are we bound
Yet never confined
Or bordered,
Given over to carelessness,
Deceived nor lost.
Forever freely given
And in like kind
Do we learn to give.
We cannot help it.
This is our way
And in insurmountable joy
Do we press on,
Relentless in the leisure
Of our surrender
To perpetual freedom alive.
Alive, alive
To all the wonderous possibilities
Before us, placed there
By ourselves and
Our Creator
In concert together
Beyond all possible thought
Of separation that
Even the word together
Could contain.

## III

Held fast by this delicate thread
Am I, unwilling to even
Contemplate escape.
For where away
Am I to travel?
There is no place outside real
That I care to go
No glitter attracts me
No wrapper I wish to unmend.

No longer am I held captive
To an audience
Bereft of imagination.
Mine is of the leaves
Blown perpetual into fall
And scattered to the lost worlds found
Where forever is renewed
With just a smile,
Behind the eye,
Who twines, the golden thread.

# Lost And Found Reflection Among The Petroglyphs

aving not gone anywhere after all
Through discovery of living change,
At first glance
Not much has moved
Here in the high desert
Where I was born.
Fifty seven years.
With my absence,
I look closely
At the untamed contortions
Of the undulant
Tree mottled terrain
Sprawled hundreds of miles
Across the sun swept silence
For any sign or signal
Of earthly progress.
But what is there here
To expect
In a land whose last
Mighty upheaval, occurred
Fifty five million years ago
And whose rains can be counted
In handfuls of drops.
Standing at the base
Of these majestic books,
Their patinaed cliffs

Rising rampart abrupt
And carving rugged lines
In the cobalt blue,
I am the sun's own spelunker
Submerged in the truth
There is ultimately no such thing
As time.
The total quiet invades
My being,
Crashing through the remnant
Of tumbled imaginary walls
Who once confined
A fragile smallness
Where a terrified uselessness
Tried to hide.
Gratefully standing
In the steep slide of mancos shale,
Gazing at outcroppings
That hold fist sized clams
Fossilized along with
Bacalites and ammonites,
The sounds of my ancestors
Come dancing dancing
Passing by in the dust brown red
That is raised by their memory
As it slams me fast
Eye to eye
With the countless few
Who also recognize
We are brothers and more
In an ageless
Continuous vertical legend
That is going on all at once,
Everywhere.
Without becoming labored
With a frozen past

Or chained to a slavery
Of ideals,
I realize I am set free
From the fetters
Of a slow time self
Confined to comparison
And judgement, jaded
By the ineptitude
Of anything so myopic
As the supposed finality of death
And its attendant body of dogma.
The pungent fragrance
Of juniper mixed
With highland sage
Wakes me aware
To the scent of antelope free
And my reflection
In the eye of their fragrant clarity.
Our song is fired
Of the same spirit
As are the bones
That hold up these mountains.
And even though
The air is absolutely still
And not one great wing
Can be seen plying
The vacuum of blue
Above the rangy towers,
I hear the multitudes singing
All around eon upon age,
Bracketed by unhurried deliberate waves
That rearrange the sand worn fine
Bordering the long gone ancient lake
Who more than once
Covered this land
On just such a wonderful day

As this.
If anything,
The stunted junipers
Seem smaller
Like it's their lot
To shrink somehow
And cause the gnarled trunks
Who support the highly successful
Leafy green pediculed design
To appear less than grandiose;
But this, is only another illusion
Of my own.
I was little more than
A foot tall then.
Everything was bigger than I.
I still remember the Presence,
And the loving warmth
Of His benefit
As He constantly surrounds me
Punctuated by spur of the moment visits
Of the Presence itself
And His entourage
Riding upon an invisible cloud
Of wisdom.
One visit in particular
Comes to mind
As it occurred
While I sat naked
Playing in the mud
Created by my own sacred urine
Mixed with the dull red dust.
Gramm had picked me up
Just then,
And gone to rinse me off
In my very own
Shallow flatrock basin nearby

Full of the sky's tears
Who pictured perfectly
The grey bottomed
White mountains
That run free
In their majestic
Sea of blue.
I looked up into gramm's
Ageless eyes
As she answers yes,
She sees Him too.
Apparently, it is time for my nap
In the shade of a favorite elder
Upon the homespun woolen saddle
Blanket borrowed from Gingie,
Aunt Louise's spunky mustang.
It smells strong
Of his stained sweat
And some of his loose hairs
Tickle my face
But that just makes it all
The more comforting
Cradled here
By the surrounding
Above ground roots
Long worn smooth
By the furs and hides
That swaddled family
As far back as infant gramm
And beyond.
The ancient juniper
Who is as much a parent
To me as anyone,
Sings the softest of lullabies
That endures unworn to this day
With the unconquerable strength

Of our stellar beginnings
Long before
A self imposed separation.
The purest essence of this
Branch laden symphony
Rejoices in
The blessedness of miracles
And caresses
The monumental moment
Where they are no longer needed,
As well.
No eye, no matter
How heavy lidded
Can ever be clouded
Upon remembrance
Of awakening from
The dream within the dream,
Which in and of itself is but a dream,
That last stop
Before becoming
The singular reality
Of love
Who has been my silent companion
All along waiting patiently
For the one thing
It did not possess
My embrace.
I awaken gently
From my nap,
Some fifty seven years later
Here among the shaded
Familiar roots
Of my beloved ancestor,
Refreshed absolutely
In the arms of my loving Father,
For, I am come home.

# My War My Peace

ccurs in a place
Seemingly in a world
That won't go away;
Yet, I know that it does
When I look in the face
Of wonderous Love.

The miracle is mine
As I give it today.
Yours to keep
Near your heart should you
Fall short in the way,
Of beautiful Love.

But war is my folly
I'm wont to demise;
I hear my rage darken
An old fam'ly door,
Veil to the holy
Garden of Love.

There's no one here.
Not evening's shadow
Or a long waited wave
Nor a spell cast
By a gossamer tear
Know of my singular Love.

From all dead thoughts
Would I fly far away

To where the cold hands
Can't cover
That which is sought
My precious Love.

And so I surrender
The good with the bad
Knowing the lost
Cannot leave me
'Til I remember
My Father's One Love.

My peace has no boundary
Nor a shinier better
When old heart's made new
In the midst of illusion's despair.
At impeccable foundry
O brilliant is Love.

To brilliance beyond
My darkness is done.
Burned clean is my will
And aligned with His own.
I vanish in song
Found at home here in Love
Where forgotten, is gone.

# Outlaws At Last

Scene: *a medium sized small town somewhere*
*in the Midwest. It is a sunny, cotton ball cloud*
*kind of day, accompanied by a warm breeze turned*
*hot that wants to share itself with everyone.*

Can you tell me where
I might fit in?
I'm kinda new
Here in town
And don't know
My way around
Just yet.
All these straight
Line streets
Criss-cross my mind
And I'm not used to
Such sleepful
Regimentation.
I gather you most likely
Think I wander
With a sidewinder motion,
But really it's only
My prairie ways,
Not just an incoherent
Shortcut to rudeness.
I'm a fair hand
At conscience
And am more than willing
To play straight up
With you

If you're of a mind
To do the same.
My six shooter
Is of a rare polish
As it is slow to anger.
With a patient saddle
I'm bended
With a whip I can't
Be broke.
'Tis a rocky trail
I've ever known
But  I'm surefooted
And even slower to spook.
The twists and turns
Of a dark lit way
Have challenge
By the tail,
But I hold the handle
To his heart, gently.
The answer in truth
Without fail, works its way
To the top of the pile
Where the harvest is rich
Always because
The roots run so deep.
I'm not from around here.
Not from my drawl
Can you tell where I hail,
But rather
From my manner.
I'm old style
Been around the mountain.
Not that age is especially
Anything to brag about,
But experience has
Its share of ease,

Sort of like old money.
Most probably
Respectability
Would make my best foil,
But I'd rather sit here
In the shade of your
Back porch
And listen to your daughter
All full of sass
And perky ambition.
Never mind
Her daddy owns
The bank
And just about
Everything else
Hereabouts.
I don't want his money
It's all confounded
With worry
And all bloody
With high pressure.
Nope.
His daughter will do
Just fine.
Her turned up little nose
Is pink-red on the end
Where the sun has burned it
Some,
But I don't mind
As I love
The way she wrinkles it
Over her glass
Of cool lemonade.
I guess she finds me
Exciting,
Dressed in my country way

Covered with dust.
Or perhaps she is bored
With city life
And her dapper beaus,
All lifeless with their
Yes ma'ams and scented hankies.
Could it be
I'm being taken for a ride?
She says she's eighteen,
But I know otherwise.
Sixteen is more like it.
Boldly, I ask her
What she wants out of life.
A husband? House? Family?
She blushes but holds
My gaze steady,
Determined to be
Both knowledgeful
And wise.
Her want is to travel
Far and wide.
Done for now
Is she of everyday same.
Nothing of the incurious
Can keep her interest
And for some time now
She has been restless
Without knowing why.
The hot midsummer breeze
Pushes the hands
Around to two o'clock
As the towered timepiece
Down the way
Moans a lackluster pm.
I can feel her sense
Of frustration

Here in the land
Of nowhere
With its recalcitrant
Nothing going on,
And I have compassion
For her
No, both of us.
I can sense the trap
Close around life
With a deadening thump
As she shivers chill
In the cold lie.
I want to comfort her
For she thinks she is alone
In this world that offers
No escape from convention,
But she would only shy
Away at my approach.
I talk her down instead,
Easing her sudden fear
In discovery
That we are somewhat
Alike.
She softens,
And that nervous
Little twitch
At the corners of her mouth
Subsides
And that look,
Of hope springs eternal,
Brightens her sweet face
The way a sleepy pup
Wanders out from under
A spring wagon
Woken abruptly
From its nap.

---

She is more observant
Than I first gave her
Credit for
And my esteem
Readjusts itself
Momentarily.
Something moves
Deep inside of me
Suddenly
And I'm made to feel
Somewhat uncomfortable,
Or is it maybe
A little scared.
She feels it too,
And glances down quickly
At her fancy
Tailor-made boots
I don't know,
Perhaps embarrassed
At the way
Her own heart
So flagrantly
Runs away from the bit
Tossing its mane
Carelessly wild.
With timeless fingertips
I and I see that I am
Made for each other;
Echoes of a broader range
Of knowing
Than what this small spectrum
Of almost
Can offer.
There is so much to share
If I can just keep ourselves
From stealing

What God freely gives.
So, it's agreed then.
I and I silently sign
Our new covenant
To honor and obey
The one real love
That  cannot be held separate
Or for that matter,
Held at all.
I instead, embrace each other
As the singular perfection
I truly am
And rejoice
In the proof
That as far as this shadow world
Is concerned,
We are outlaws,
At last.

# Country Boy

pider in the shadow
With no echo to his name
Cries out to his Father's Light
That one enduring flame

A given spark to me below
That swallows all my pain
Keeps returning to my limpid sight
And burns away the shame

He knows not the web I wove
Nor that from him did I refrain
I'm always kept within His mind of might
Where I am born again

I gave up hunting long ago
Run away thoughts in train
No longer fearful of darkness blight
With truth I shall remain

No more plight does hubbub show
Upon a wasted plain
For never will love prove contrite
Love can find no blame

My Father's house has room for me
Any corner may I choose
And if I wish a sunny pleasant beach
He's got many I can use

No more webs need I see
I have nothing left to lose
Only learn from what I have to teach
And laugh away the blues

It's all in what I do believe
There is nothing to peruse
I have honest peace within my reach
And no more double two's

I thank the lack You relieve
Rob me of my snooze
Sing love's lovely song each to each
Rightly spread the news

It's all done I do receive
This love I do know Whose
There is no need of windy speech
Or stones to fill my shoes

I love the little brook
That runs between my toes
It sings merrily without a care
As along it simply flows

I cannot help the way I look
The sun has burned my nose
To you this love I freely share
As the mud it stains my clothes

Trees shade this bowered nook
Where freedom freely goes
Struck dumb I gawk and stare
At my blood the sap it crows

Reason for this trip I took
How reasonable the love it shows
Is all the food I need prepare
The breeze it gently blows

And now I bless what I forsook
About time goodness knows
And all that trundles under bridge to scare
Are only tipsy trolls

It's now time for no time
I'm being lifted up
The way a delighted birthday child
Picks out a newborn pup

In my Father's hand sublime
I watch Him fill my cup
While handspring heart goes simply wild
Ol' never has had enough

Love is an easy rhyme
Fear is loathe to sup
And to lost oblivion long defiled
Truth can play too rough

Forgiveness of my crime
Is my first job to tally up
And a given tone will prove right mild
When short can feel abrupt

Looked for forgetful now's in line
To be used and loosely cut
The way earthly memories sorely trialed
Little flame, goes sputter sputter sput

# Broken Mystery

cannot find
Where I began
Perhaps I never started.
There is no answer
In the chaff
The seeds
Have all departed.
With no beginning
There can be no end
But what about
The middle?
The slowest
Is the fast
The biggest
Is the small,
I'm sure the answer
To the twist
Does not exist
At all.
(There is no twist)

<u>II</u>
When I look
Through eyes
That do not see
Ears
That cannot hear,
The voice
That cannot touch
Another's heart

Forever is unclear.
When I look with
Fingers
That do not feel
Feet
That step alone,
And
Wings who cannot
Swim the sky
I'm want to give
It all away,
This phantom
Music's drone.

III
I let me go
To fall away
With the snow
That forever
Burns the sun,
For the drunken loss
Of a loser's mask
Whose strings
Have come undone,
This forgiveness real
Which is too hot
For cool conceal
Puts all dark lovers
On the run,
And though they're fast
Death cannot outlast
The loving arms
Of our only One.

# Faith, Hope And Love

y footsteps fall silently
As they touch a forest floor softly,
Unnoticed by landed eyes.
I have them shut, grateful for the latitude
Trust brings when I am within my own
beauty.
The trees are singing.
No longer do they withhold meaning from me
Their little voyeur, who is free to wander
Among grizzled trunks
For he knows that they are his own.
Every root and hanging branch.
All is shared.
Even the dried and tumbled snags chorus true,
If but faintly.
At first glance a natural might say
The listeners are trapped night after night,
Day after day, hour in, hour out, all festooned in their
Mosses green and lichens scarlet red with gold
And purple fringe
Impounded by the fallen notes
Each one true to its leafy splendor.
But in truth, none of the music is marked by time.
I feel my gravity disappear,
Losing its mundane oppressiveness
For herein abides my freedom to express all boundless joy
Liberated from the shackles of sleep induced frenzies.
Solitude to me does not mean alone or
Necessarily tolerant to silence.
More like free to enjoy more of that which comes to mind.

That is why I need it, this moment in now.
A place to readjust interactive clamor
And listen to the few words I am able to hear
From my master.
A few choice words from the day's lesson
Taken to heart, drowning the desert surround
With their certainty of step by steps
Echoed by the trees.
Even in the night my forest is grand.
Taunted by her moon dappled fragrances
I am easy prey;
Having learned love resists not I am bent on
Adaptation which is always successful
After miseries are forgotten for the mirages they really are.
Perfect happiness for me is my Father's Will.
Complete, unabridged and lovingly accepted.
Furthermore, nothing is impossible.
Even that which cannot happen in a conventional world.
Like me, a silly old bear who wants so much to fly.
For me. For her.
I love a little bird.
And determined, I tearfully told her today
Hoping our nests could be joined together.
But bears this bear, doesn't sleep in trees
And birds don't nest in dens.
Now I am my unqualified self again;
Not so much to fly
But to be love,
So that someday I can whisper in her tiny ear
I too dance upon the water.

# Lamb Takes Lion

n the chimera
Where darkness
Reigns supreme
I win the war
That never seems
To end
By failing
To resist.
Oh, it's a bloody
Mess all right.
Hell is always
On fire
With a flame
That is like
A bad piece
Of meat.
The more you
Chew it, the
Bigger it gets.
Fortunately,
I wasn't
Hungry.
Somehow I'm
Finding my way
Outta here.
At least that's
The way it is
Being made
To look.
I promise you,

As to what
Is going on
I don't have
A clue.
I do know
I want to go
Home.
I heard about
Some kind of
Door that
Isn't there
But looks like
A wall instead.
It must be
A wall I made,
Because I made it.
Maybe this door
Is somewhere
Behind me or inside,
Lost in shadows
Or covered up
With old lies.
It would be
The kind of thing
I'd bring
With me to forget
So I could find it.
Apparently, I like
To scare myself.
Well I've really
Gone and done it
This time.
Neither the good
Nor the bad holds
A way out.
As a matter of fact

Good and bad
Are more like
Interchangeable labels
Depending on which
Side of the pitchfork
I get up on.
I knew I was
In trouble
The minute
I signed up for
Military intelligence.
I'd accidentally
Spelled it wrong
But nobody noticed.
They used to hammer
Into us this thing
About careers
And wallet longevity
But I could never seem
To fit in.
I was more interested
In doing a good job
And having fun
While I was doing it.
As the promotions
Came around
I was always passed by
In favor of some chap
Who had just
Screwed things up
Royal torrey.
I guess they needed
Some place to put him.
They said a promotion
Was always the way up,
But it looked like

Down to me.
The poor gipp
Was made to dress
And act like them
And pretty soon
You couldn't
Tell them apart.
Yep, he was being
Punished for sure.
What tipped me off
Was the fact that
They would never
Say exactly who
They were.
Sounded kind of
Like they were
Harshly potty trained
And had something
To hide.
Anyway, pretty soon
I noticed I was
Being ignored
And increasingly
Left on my own.
The bus stops kept
Getting further apart
And there were
Fewer and fewer
Passengers.
We didn't appear
To have much
In common
On the outside
But it was obvious
That when it came
To fitting in with

Status quo
We didn't know
If we'd been shot
Skunked
Or snake bit.
After a while,
Being left alone
Became a full time
Responsibility
That accorded some kind
Of autonomy
Which always scares
Those who leave
The important stuff
Up to somebody else,
And so we were made
Quasi respectable.
We were feared
And trusted
At the same time.
I don't know how
In hell they
Came up with that
Combination
But now that I look back
On it, it makes sense
In an insane sort of way.
Every once in a while
Someone would breech
Out by the front door
And right away
We would put them
In charge.
If the new soul
Couldn't speak English,
All the better.
Meanwhile, we
Continued to give

Everything away
Which scared
The hell out of the matrix.
They thought we had
The plague
But actually
The information
Was all about
More effective ways
To dump your garbage
And leave a clean mess
While you were doing it.
When they found out
There wasn't any
Money in it
They lost interest
Right away saying
Our project didn't
Have a future.
They wanted tangible
Evidence but our
Fearless leader
Said it was pretty hard
To put a tattoo
On smoke,
But instead they
Should surrender
What piss little
They amounted to
On their own
And accept soon
As possible
All the love
In the universe
And then some.
It is free too
And you are always
Welcome to come

Back for seconds
And thirds.
Just remember
To give it all away.
That's how to
Make more.
One smart ass
Wanted to know
If the universe
Wouldn't get just
A little crowded
But I clued him in
Saying it is
A pretty big place
And it just so
Happens that love
Is what everything
Is made of anyway
And if it does
Fill up we'll
Add on.
That clown must
Have been one
Of mine.
Anyway, as you all
Know by now
We got to laughin'
So hard we fell
Through that door
In the wall
That wasn't there
And now it's gettin'
So I can't remember
What I was so scared
About.
Want to do it
Again?

# Lover Be Loved

The Gorgon's head
Tries to raise its eyes
My sun wins out instead,
And all the wing'ed wonders fair
Sing sweet songs
That fill the air
Forgiving the hurts I've bled.
For what purpose
Other should I see it through
There is only truth,
To be and do.
My course is set
I'm going home
Now with intentions true;
Blessed
For being no more than willing,
Am I able to pursue.
I can feel a mighty hand
In all of this
My story here with you;
I'm so glad to touch your heart
With mine
To finally know my love,
And have it drown me
In my Father's light
That shines down
From up above.

<u>II</u>

The lonely whine
Of not enough
Withers before the dawn
While joy sparkles at the dancing feet
Of Pan's own scamper faun;
Who dares to be equal
To my brother's keep
Who has been here
All along,
And never guesses at my sleep
Or to where I might of gone.

<u>III</u>

My mother's round face
Kisses the hills nearby
With a silvery satin sheen,
While the blessings pile high
In a warm laughing sky
Hereabouts so rarely seen.
The singing rails
And salt covered sails
Join together
For their final run home,
And this our season to sing
As our lovers take wing
Fills the glass ball
In my Father's great hall,
'Til nothing is left, in between.

# For Rosie:
# There Is A Kazoo In My Sock

All eyes
For the highland path
I'll need more to avoid
The mountain's wrath
My walk alone
Will soon be past
Because of knowing not
The die is cast
No time left for tears
To fall so fast
Or clumsy ways becalm
A lilting mast
Seas of pleasure
Robbed of youthful task
Gone now is the pain
That never felt
To be home's domain
Unlike uncertain
Dark's refrain
I'm made anew
In wonder's charm
Where the child of God
Is free of false alarm
And a cubic light year
If there ever could be
Such a thing
Would be only
A drop in the bucket.

A daring life
So I've been told
Is to live forever
Without getting old
Minus fleas and ticks
And ostentatious mold
Or friendless days
Curbed by lonely nights
And all other sorts
Of clubbed insights
That try to make nothing at all
Into something right
So that illusion's roar
Will seem more real
And diversion's cold hand
Is seen to feel
While hiding the fact
That it cannot heal
Or even come close
To the eternal light
Which would burn it serene
To my true heart's delight
And clear my wicked sight
Of its dead pursuit
Stuck in a lifeless world
As if there could ever be
Such a thing
As a private dream.

I stand here naked
The only one
As God's own creature
I outshine the sun
While fortune's kiss
Turns into shooting stars
That hair the head

Fair in the eye
Of this beholder
I look yet again
In a sky become bolder
Impossible to fright
Unable to grow older
I am given to rest
Upon daphine breast
To sleep the real life
Awakened forever
And loved
From anchor to rudder
Hell wasn't so clever
The truth brought along
Became untangled uncovered
Showing now is uncluttered
And my heart
Rings true
To its One and only
As if there could ever be
Anything else.

And now I bow before Him
Precious in my own sight as well
Most grateful to gumption
Given to swell
An impossible moment
Where sincerity befell
A soul forgotten to hope
So it could rise once again
And with the Father elope
In boundless laughter's own plan
Creating together
With all-perfect élan
The peace of a lifetime
With no beginning or end

Upside nor downside
Or middle to mend
Only life full of love
Wherever He goes;
To everywhere and nowhere
Even to nothing which already knows
The ebb of His tide
When the horn blows.

# Easter Vigil

I remain awake this night
Out of respect
For He who has never left me.
It is so little that I do.
Mostly I ignore our Father
For I am denser than stone,
Appalled at my inability to bend
And render myself to much
In the way of service
Even in my own behalf.
I watch the opportunities go by
Frantic in the midst
Of the blank paralysis
Which encodes my losses
In the annals of battles
So outrageous
No shame could ever bury.
I am joined by a small
Brown bat
Who has flown in through
An open window
To investigate
My warm reading lamp,
Hopeful of a meal.
Having forgotten the location
Of his exit,
He flies around in circles
Looking for a way out.
Nervously, he brushes the walls
With his wings.

Again and again he circles the room.
I hold still,
Pretending not to notice him
But to no avail.
He knows I'm here
Next to the lamp.
I think he has surmised
I mean him no harm
And lands on the shelf
Of the open closet
Amid the small piles
Of neatly folded clothes.
He is welcome to stay
As it has started to rain again.
The raindrops fall loudly
Upon the ground which is still cool
From winter's grasp
Even though the calendar says
It's early spring.
There won't be much about
This night
For him to catch on the fly.
He is welcome to the bread crumbs
In the bird feeder
Which would show him his freedom
But instead closes his tiny eyes,
Too tired to care.
I am comforted by him
As he breaks the monotony
But not the near silence
That surrounds us.
Perhaps this is my chance
To do something for another.
How perfect.
I shall do nothing to disturb
My tiny guest

Other than be.
That's it!
I shall just be.
Here.
Now.
Happy.
That is my new job.
It involves diligent effort,
but I need not go into that now.
The rain picks up
Its resonant beat
And I can hear the little streamlet
Run down the hill
Next to the curb if there was one.
An intermittent hail
Takes up its own cacophony
Increasing the night's rhythm
But soon fades
For lack of sufficient cold air
It could call a nursery.
That is okay.
The rain, gentle now
Has the runoff in
To lead with its busy story
Describing small rolling pebbles
Mixed with sand and mud, old leaves,
Twigs and nomadic earthworms
Who wriggle for higher ground,
Ecstatic over the coming increase
Of sustenance
At their end of the food chain.
And I am free,
Having somewhere forgiven myself.
Maybe next to the truth
That I am created whole and perfect
And need no justification

For anything.
It is my birthright yes,
As well as the rock
Upon which my foundation is laid.
And who knows how much more,
There, to be walls and roof
Open doors and windows to let in the light
And yea, I am the altar
Who brings forth the light
From within.
And to my Father I say also
To me let it come in.
I thirst mightily
And yet know not how to drink
That which is my portion.
Let me not waste away
Before Thy loving eye.
Please help me
So that I may also say,
"It is done."
I am forever grateful
For my older big brother
Whom You so generously sent me
To be my best friend
And teacher.
I promise to try harder
And do more to help myself
So that I, too, can someday hear,
"This is my son
In whom I am well pleased."
Please help me.
I can no longer stand
To be afraid of you.
Thank you.
Amen.

# Dark A Rain

ark rain
In silent puddles
Outlined by
A sleeping street's
Jaundiced light
Holds no mystery
Or curse of fright
For the instant
Freedom
Of my heart's delight
Nor can it dampen
My will to feel
The truth that lives
Inside these veins
That never fights
A slant refrain
Spawned
By lightning's roar.
No blindness touches
My swollen heart
No pain
Can harm
My mended way
The instant
I seek
No other.
Quiet of night
Bares no yellow
Dragon's tooth;
Neither can
The hiss
Of falling idols

Scare a straightened child
When he knows
There is
No death
Or possibility
Of a battle won
Only,
To be replaced
By another day
Of futility.
That which
Is not real
Cannot hurt me.
Its delay fades
Before the golden light
Of the loving,
Patient hand
That protects me always,
From myself.
Dark waters
Absorbed
By the timeless
Field
Are never lost
Even to
The last drop
For yes
Their beauty
Is recognized
As completion
Of the oft
Converted puzzle
And their precious wet
Is so highly prized
For its little willingness
To be,
Not so dark a rain.

# Uncle Louie

e's a character
My Uncle Louie.
Most of the family
Just call him
Fats.
Wild and fun loving,
Unpredictable –
That's Louie.
It was Louie
Who taught me
The delicious headiness
Of taking chances.
The family still
Loves him
In spite of his
Carefree ways
And even though
There is occasional
Interfamily grumbling,
No one complains
About his handiwork
Come spring
Roundup,
Or harvest.
He is the only one
In the family
Who can heave
A three wire bale
Up into the hayloft
From the ground

All day.
Louie was never
Much good at
The 'in between part'
Of ranchin' and farmin'
As he called it.
Too much standing around
While cultivating
And irrigation
For him.
Instead he would be
Off in the upper reaches
Of our tallest mountains
Or way way out
In the desert wastes
Bein' God knows what.
Louie always had
A kind word for everyone
And refused to take up
With any gossip.
When he was around
The ranch
Or on the trail with us
He always without fail
Had time to listen
To me
And offer comfort.
His brand of wisdom
Included a common sense
Usefulness
The years
That stretched on
Season after season
Never outgrew.
After I was near grown,
Louie took me out

One night
On the spur of the
Moment
To visit a few friends
Of his –
Some ladies
Of the evening.
They were all soft
With rosy cheeks
And glad to see
Louie.
He told them
I was his nephew
And would they mind
Shortening
My horns a little.
Later on,
Back in the parlor
We were all sitting around
As it was a "slow night,"
And while Louie was
Smoking a cigar
And dipping it in
A glass of brandy
I had occasion
To discover how he
Generously extended
Courtesy
To everyone present.
Years later,
I realize Louie
Was merely reintroducing
Everyone
To their own integrity.
Their own bless'ed
Self esteem.

Louie just has a way
Of showing you
Your own beauty
That's always been
Right there
Plain as the nose
On your face.
Anyway, all this
Flashed through my mind
As I picked up the phone
And heard:
"Hey, pardner!
Is that you?"
"Louie, is that you?"
"Yeah," came the reply,
The sound of his voice
All rough and raspy.
"Hey kid,
What cher up to?
Granny says you
Got religion
An' run off
To Wisconsin
An' joined up with
Some cult.
You ain't turned into
One o' them
Devil worshipers
Have you?"
"No, Louie, I ain't,"
I said, thinkin'
I'm goin' to have to
Explain myself
All over again.
"It ain't no
Suicide cult

Yer mixed up with?"
"No Louie,
Nothin' like that.
I'm attending a bonafide
Academy – a school
That studies exactly
What Jesus says
And how to apply it
In all our daily lives.
It isn't a religion
But a mind training."
I heard a satisfied "Oh,"
On the other end.
His country radio
Was playing in the background,
Something to the tune
Of a satisfied mind.
I can't explain it,
But I know Louie
Understood.
"How's it goin' for ya?"
'Tough at first," I said,
"But I'm starting
To get the hang of it
Now.
I'll be glad to send you
Some booklets and a video
If you want."
"Okay, but first, tell me
Some of what you've learned."
"Well, not in so many
Words am I good at
Saying it yet,
But do you remember
When you used to tell me
About standin' with one foot

On each side of
The Continental Divide
Way up in the Rockies
And how you felt
About being
So close to
God,
You know, like
He is all around
You
And you can hear
Each other's
Heartbeat
And the sky is so clear
An' you are so high up
You can see
All the way into
Nevada to the west
An' clear acrost
Nebraska an' Kansas
To the east
And it all gives you
A freedom
That can't be found
Back down in town
An' how the warm
Night wind that finds you
Curled up by campfire
And how it sings to you
The love of the land
Even in what other folks
Call lonely desert?
And how 'about that time
In the boat
Out on the lake
When I fell in

An' all the 'gators
Was alert
To come an' get me
But they backed off
When you stood up
And they saw it was you?
You said that was because
There was a light
All 'round us
But there weren't
No moon?
All these are miracles
And I see them every day.
Not a moment goes by
But what I see
Something good
Happen to people.
Sometimes there are tears
Of regret for a moment
But soon they are
Replaced
By the truth.
I know that's what
It's got to be
'Cause all of a sudden
I can see for myself
They have been
Set free
And I'm included."
There is a silence
From Louie's end
And then I hear
Him ask
"So what's this place
You're at
Do they call it?"

"It's called the Endeavor Academy."
I thought about my answer for a moment
Trying to think
Of the best way
To describe
The most wonderful place
I ever been in
And I remember
Uncle Louie
Has spent no small
Amount of time
Behind bars for D.E.U.I.
Doing everything while
Under the influence,
And it occurs to me
To say for the
Maximum benefit of
His understanding
"The academy is an
Alternative
Correctional facility."
"Are you going to be
Getting out soon?"
He wants to know.
"We're all going home
Any day now, I reply."
"Good," says Louie.
"You have my blessing, kid.
See you in the stars!"

# God's Own Gypsy

God's own gypsy steps through the night
    upon the path
Of a bowered vale and over brook
    benign of wrath
To love's campfire, bright with fiddler's rune
His breast filled to burst this mesmer tune
And how it returns for more so soon
This thief of blight one more, full moon.

With silvered clouds reclined upon far silent hills
Horned owl calls out and gives the scurries chills
Who scamper about the sanded dunes,
Bunched with spearsharp grass.
I remark the wave who breaks
The calm smooth sea of glass
My voice, used by the word that has come to pass
As the angels amazed,
Own their joy for He has come, has come at last.

Now I rise to occasion in boundless cheer
Knowing there is no longer anything to fear
For I'm free to go this very night
I am love's companion bright.
No longer restrained and kept hidden from sight
By illusions shame and backwards plight
I am my Father's flame, His one embraced delight.

Oh gypsy, gypsy grown so bold
I'm glad to see you've spurned the cold
And heard the bell for it is rung
For all of you has it always sung
And now at last you are among
The rest of you, remained so young.

Glory's sun does rise, and puts a gleam into my eyes
As it shoots through naked branch to fill the skies
And burn the little fog on thither pond
While geese arrive soon from gone beyond
Where God's peace makes true the icy frond
Of black tree who points my home, where I belong.

A gathered cloud tries to break away
From humble crag who begs his brother stay
And save him for the coming year
To greet together all melted tears
Who now crystal spritely in the night but not in fear
For Father's son in truth, is always with me here.

Mother doe upon the hill among sleeping trees
Who grow like hair,
Calls to buck a loving dare,
Please come and dance without a care.
Our feet the fallen leaves we'll share, as bard
Sings out for all to spare this wooded ward
And give each to all our wedded bridge toward
Knowing heaven is home to all, who trudge without regard.

Oh, gypsy, gypsy, thy word is love
Behold the dawn as I kiss the dove
For in your sweetheart's arms awake
And gift yourself this moment take.
Now is forever without a break,
Why I pray You Father, my soul to slake.

The withered leaves have left their trees
And resting upon the floor, now take their ease
As I watch empty branches scrape our sky
Whose marestail clouds declare,
Storm a soon be passing by.
To cover a blue grown chill with northern sigh
Is like having love, without ever need of knowing why.

Ten turkeys grouse the yard for burrowed sunshine seed
While ladybugs invite themselves
Herewith into my room full speed
To beat the cold of a quiet day and there, sleep it all away.
I am welcomed here into their home
Where I may freely play,
T'was theirs long before my ancestors' hair
Found it could turn grey
And longer still before the end began,
It just works out that way.

When I came out before I went in
Is how I beat upcoming sin.
The poor beggar never had a chance
For it was out before all out was in.
And that is how I returned back home without I ever left,
A laugh came along and burned it all
And made no gloom bereft.
So no pirate had a treasure he could bury in a chest
And I had no reason not to sing for joy, love can do no less.

Oh, gypsy, gypsy, t'was all foretold
You never could have gotten old
Or forgotten your Father's song
Or planned to play all night alone
With separate heart who's never strong
I love you now, love's never wrong.